THE
AWAKENING
OF
WASHINGTON'S
CHURCH

The

AWAKENING

of

WASHINGTON'S
CHURCH

How a church lost everything

and gained what matters most

J.B. SIMMONS

All royalties from this book will be donated to The Falls Church Anglican. To learn more about the author, visit www.jbsimmons.com.

All Scripture quotations, unless otherwise indicated, are taken from the Holy Bible, English Standard Version.

Cover design by Liana Moisescu.

ISBN: 978-1530686911

Printed in the United States of America

CONTENTS

Not long ago a historic church in Virginia took a stand for its faith and lost everything—its priceless property that George Washington had graced, its entire savings, even its communion silver. But the church did not fade. It had been pruned of material things. It was ready to grow and thrive as never before, planting new churches and proclaiming the Gospel of Jesus Christ.

This church's experience has echoed throughout the world. Somehow the story of its stand and its losses caught the imagination of people and the attention of the press near and far. Biblical faith faces persecution but promises eternal reward, as it always has. Times of cultural drift call for renewal and awakening. They call for powerful stories of God's sovereign work. This is one of those stories.

This is the story of The Falls Church Anglican.

AUTHOR'S NOTE

Big religious ideas can make my faith falter. Theologies about prayer don't solve my deepest questions. Concepts like free will and election remain mysteries. I try to use logic to understand these things, and I don't make it very far. Then I fall back to a childlike memory: *because the Bible tells me so.*

But is that enough? Thankfully, God gives us another kind of answer. He gives us stories.

About a year before I started writing this book, an idea popped into my head. Every Sunday as I left church I felt a pull to write a story about what was going on there. I told my wife about this tugging. She told me to follow it, pray about it.

But I write fiction, I would say, *not books about churches.* I tried to shake the feeling. It wouldn't let me go.

After a year of this, I took a small step forward: I invited John and Susan Yates over for lunch. I'd never talked to them in person like this, but I needed to tell them about my idea. We were halfway into a salmon salad when I launched into it.

John listened, nodded knowingly, and then said: *About a year ago, I started praying for someone to write a book about our church. Maybe you're the one.*

And so this book was born.

We don't need theology to tell us whether God answers prayers. He gives us stories.

ACKNOWLEDGMENTS

One thing should be clear from the beginning: the story of this church is not about a building. It's about people. It's about changed lives. From George Washington to John Yates, leaders of this church have reflected a light that the nation, and the world, wanted to follow. The secret to this light is that it wasn't their own. They were humble leaders who shared what God had given them. They inspired this story, and so this book would not exist without them.

Nor would the book exist without the many people at The Falls Church Anglican who gave their time to speak with me. I interviewed dozens of people. Some are named in these pages, some not, but you'll hear all their voices. Each has added perspective and truth. Their ages ranged from 28 to 94. They included: Susan Yates, Frances Long, Virginia Watson, Al and Jean Trakowski, Don and Angela Dusenberry, Mark and Katherine Weller, Rich Dean, Martha Cole, Sam and Judy Thomsen, Robert Watkin, Nicholas Lubelfeld, Dan Henneberg, Mike and Elizabeth Brunner, Allison Gaskins, George Hooper, Steve and Nancy Skancke, Hugo Blankingship, Charlie Powell, Howard and Molly Shafferman, Morna and Chris Comeau, Scott Ward, Steffen Johnson, Sam Ferguson, and Dan Marotta. Thanks also go to Michael Anderson and Daniel Murphy for their honest and insightful editing, and to Lindsay Simmons, a better first reader and life partner than I could ever deserve.

I would have loved to interview George Washington. The best I could do was a few biographies. These resources and other information about this book's sources are provided in the end notes. Another piece of the history is from my own. Family tradition holds that one of my ancestors is John Trammell, the man who gave the church its two-acre property in 1746.

The greatest pleasure of my work on this book was sitting down multiple times to talk with John Yates. Writing this book is an honor, because it includes so many of his wise words. Thank you, John, for loving us and inspiring us. You taught me how to mature as a man and as a believer. You helped me become the kind of person who could write this book.

All of the sermons and programs at the church would mean little if they didn't change people's lives. But they did. We should heed the words recounted in this book from the pulpit of The Falls Church, because those words derive from the Word, and the Word gives life.

FOREWORD BY JOHN YATES

I am extremely grateful to my friend, the indefatigable J.B. Simmons, for heeding God's prompting to write this story. For some time I have believed that it's a story that needs to be told, not simply because wherever we go people ask us what's happened, but also because in several ways our story is the story of so many other congregations seeking to be faithful to God and to his holy word in a revisionist age. The places, people, and details differ but countless churches across the spectrum of Protestantism in the early 21st century have weathered similar experiences and have been learning lessons similar to the ones we have learned.

My only quarrel with J.B. about the book is that my name and actions are overemphasized. The truth is that remarkable men and women have shared in the leadership of our church every step of the way and their faith and obedience and hard work have been every bit as important and essential as mine. This is a story of the body of Christ sharing in the work of Christ. I have never known a church blessed with so many gifted and committed people so willing to devote enormous amounts of time and effort to see the church thrive. It isn't unusual for a church warden here to spend twenty five hours a week in serving our church. Countless people have sensed God's call to minister in and through this church in sacrificial ways, giving hours and hours, week in and week out to Christ's work, working as hard as staff members. Our philosophy has always been that ministry is best done by volunteers and that staff are best utilized when they are serving and assisting the ministry of the people. We don't have either "professional" or "lay" workers in our church—all are called as ministers of Christ, and ministry in the home, community, office, school, and marketplace is as crucial and important as ministry within the church itself.

This book simply cannot begin to include all the inspiring stories of lives changed by the Gospel, and by the power of the Holy Spirit as

God works among us. As I have read J.B.'s account the faces and voices and stories of people who are not mentioned here are continually before me: conversations and conversions; reconciliation and renewal; healing and homes and lives actually turned around by Christ. We have seen God at work since we first arrived in Falls Church, drawing people into fellowship and enveloping them in a sense of God's presence, and opening their minds and hearts to accept the person and promises of Christ.

I have spent a good deal of time compiling lists of men and women who have been essential to the story of our church's awakening: My "Wise Men" who have met with me repeatedly over the years as counselors; friends who have loved us and believed in us and encouraged us in extraordinary ways to persevere and remain faithful; vestry leaders who have particularly stimulated me and the church to think bigger, to strive for God's highest and best in all matters; ministry leaders who have worked with unusual success to strengthen and build up the church; my study assistants who year in and year out have run errands, tracked things down, aided me in countless ways; my personal assistants who have kept track of countless relationships, meetings, making me look good and loving on the many, many people who are in our office day by day; the men who have risen at dawn or gathered weeknights after work, to study scripture with me and consider the weighty questions we all face . . . after listing literally hundreds of names I have realized that I cannot do this adequately. There are too many to be included, and so I will forgo this effort, only to say our church has been generously, unusually blessed with amazing people "of whom the world was not worthy"! It's God who has built this unusual church and I have had the privilege to be at the center of these people for 37 years.

It is imperative that I attempt to thank the churches in our region that opened their doors to us during our "tabernacling" period. The kindness and generosity of these friends enabled us to continue meeting when we had no place to call our own. The Falls Church

Episcopal—they have been wonderful in allowing us to continue to have periodic funerals and receptions there—we differ on much but they are our good friends; Columbia Baptist Church; McLean Presbyterian Church; Cornerstone Evangelical Free Church; Rivendell School; the Catholic Diocese of Arlington—St. James Church and Bishop O'Connell High School; Truro Anglican Church; Restoration Anglican; Little Falls Presbyterian; Cherrydale Baptist; St. Mary's Orthodox; First Christian Church; Holy Trinity Lutheran; Immanuel Bible Church; Vienna Presbyterian Church; McLean Bible Church; Fairfax Presbyterian; Calvary Christian Church; Culmore United Methodist; Knox Presbyterian; Capital Life Church; First Baptist Alexandria; National Presbyterian; and others I'm probably forgetting!

I will only mention one person by name and that is my best friend who has been my wife for 47 years. Susan's passion, faith, encouragement, wisdom, and ministry with me have made these years a great joy.

John Yates
Holy Week 2016

1

Prologue

Remember your leaders, those who spoke to you the word of God. Consider the outcome of their way of life, and imitate their faith.
Hebrews 13:7

It's Monday, March 28, 1763. Most of the early spring snow has melted, but a few white dustings remain on the Northern Virginia countryside. The roads are dreadfully muddy. The sky is dreadfully gray.

But the young man riding north isn't thinking about those things. He admires the farms, studying the slopes of the gentle hills, the slopes that lead down to Alexandria. He knows this land. It's home. Through the forest to his left, he spots the familiar glimmer of lake water. He's been riding since dawn. His horse has earned a drink and a rest. He tugs the reins left.

At the small lake's shore, he climbs out of the saddle and leads his horse to the water. She drinks for a while. Then he does the same. For a moment, he pauses where he kneels and glances up. The clouds reveal a few hints of blue. Maybe the sun will shine after all. He closes his eyes and thanks Providence.

He continues riding north. His thoughts drift to Martha, then to the spring tobacco planting. With a new field to plant, this year's crop might produce better. He smiles. That might allow him to build the new barn, using his own design. And maybe he could order a finer coat from London.

The church finally appears in the distance. He is muddy and tired. *Was it really worth all this to be on the vestry, to help lead a church?* But the doubt passes. His great, great grandfather was an Anglican minister. It was his faith that brought the Washingtons to America in the first place. And his mother had taught him devotion. She might be proud to see him named among this group.

George understands this will raise his stature in the community. He already has some renown. People know of his military successes . . . and defeats. They also know him as an accomplished surveyor and farmer. Now they could know him as a civil leader. This strikes George as odd—that serving a church should matter for service of the state. The two seem separate to him, but so it is under the King.

As he arrives, George ties his horse outside the old wooden church on the path to the falls. It has been standing for thirty years and has not aged well. A man named John Trammell gave two acres to the church back then. It's a fine two acres, with some nice oaks along a good road. The mud isn't so bad here, but the building needs work.

George steps inside and finds the meeting about to begin. The others greet him cordially. "Welcome, Colonel Washington." He no longer holds the rank as commander of the Virginia regiment, but he does not deny the honorary title. The group sits and begins its discussion.

At thirty-one, George is the youngest in the room, and this is his first official duty as a vestryman. He's had little formal education, much less in matters of religion, but he has learned from his daily reading of Scriptures. One lesson comes to mind: *be swift to hear, slow to speak.* So he stays quiet at the meeting's start, listening and observing.

"We must build a new church," says one man. "People hardly attended services this winter. The wind blew straight through these old plank walls. We must build with something stronger. Brick, perhaps."

"We do not have the funds for such expense," another man says. "We have many poor to care for. Our efforts are better spent improving what we have."

"I agree," says William Payne. George knows Mr. Payne, and respects him. "If we build some fine, rich church here, it belongs to the King. We shouldn't build up *his* church. We should build up the church of the Lord."

A few men shudder at that. Even George is taken aback. Men rarely flaunt the name of the Lord, much less in a disloyal utterance against the King. But George wouldn't deny Mr. Payne his passions. He had a point. *To each his own vine and fig tree.*

"Maybe we should move it," John West suggests. "The church could be in a more convenient place."

"No." Charles Broadwater plants his hands on his knees, leveling with the other men. "We must build a new house fit for worship here. James Wren can draw up the plans. He's kin to Sir Christopher Wren, who designed St. Paul's Cathedral in London. We should have a great building here. One that will stand the test of time."

"Colonel Washington," William Payne says, "what do you think?"

All eyes turn to him. George is thoughtful for a moment, then he speaks. "We have no need to compete with the King's church in London. It would lead us to vanity and vexation of the spirit. The building matters only as it serves a purpose. It is a place for the faithful to gather. It is a house of worship, and this one is rotten and unfit for repair."

William Payne nods. "So it is."

"You speak truth," another man says. "What do you think we should do?"

"We ought to use this land well," George replies. "It's good land, with fine trees. People have come to know it as a place where Providence leads. The only matter to be decided is what sort of building we might commission. I know James Wren. He's an honest man, with talent. I believe we should do as Charles suggests."

Payne is shaking his head. "But what about it being the King's property?" Payne knows that George has heard the talk of discontentment.

George doesn't shy from his friend's gaze. "Larger changes must come before we can do anything about that." He turns to address the others. "We know there will be wars and rumors of wars. But we also know the church has only one true owner. The Great Architect of the Universe will lay our plans."

The words of young George Washington sit comfortably with the group. The men talk a while longer. When the vestry draws up its minutes, they declare the old building "rotten and unfit for repair."[1]

It's time to build something new.

2

Two American Centuries

I sought for the key to the greatness and genius of America in her harbors...; in her fertile fields and boundless forests; in her rich mines and vast world commerce; in her public school system and institutions of learning. I sought for it in her democratic Congress and in her matchless Constitution. Not until I went into the churches of America and heard her pulpits flame with righteousness did I understand the secret of her genius and power.

Attributed to Alexis de Tocqueville

George Washington and the rest of the vestry at The Falls Church agreed on the plan of James Wren—Sir Christopher Wren's descendent—for a new brick building. It was a colonial adaptation of Georgian architecture, made of local red bricks. Construction was completed in 1769.

Tradition holds that the Declaration of Independence was read to local citizens from the steps of the church in 1776. It is also said that the church was a recruiting station during the Revolutionary War. With George Washington's election as the first President, the church's historic stature was firmly established in America.

History and stature, however, do not equate to faith and vibrancy. The American Revolution divided churches like The Falls Church, pitting patriots against British loyalists. Anglican clergy were required to swear allegiance to the king, as an oath of the Church of England. This led patriots to strip many Anglican parishes of their financial support. After the war, debates broke out in the Virginia legislature over church property that had been held by the Church of England.[2] While The Falls Church managed to keep its property, it lost many members and fell into neglect and disrepair for decades.

But still the building stood, and still God was at work.

A series of restorations followed. The Falls Church officially joined the Episcopal Church in 1836. Captain Henry Fairfax, grandson of Lord Fairfax, spent much of the family's fortune to restore the church's interior in 1838. Eight years later, at age 41, Henry Fairfax died in the Mexican-American War. His body was brought back to the church and buried there.

The improved building did little on its own to grow the church. When a new minister arrived in October 1842, he reported that he "found but 10 communicants and 6 families" in the church. He also listed these statistics: "Baptisms, adult 2, infant 2, total 4. Funerals 3." The church was not dead, but it was certainly quiet in those years.

The quiet ended in 1861, and not for religious reasons. Virginia seceded on May 23 and established the Confederate capital in Richmond. Union forces immediately occupied Arlington and the bridges over the Potomac. The Falls Church was caught in the middle.

By August 3, 1861, Union forces had taken the church. An article on that day included a sketch of the building and a brief history. "This is the most advanced post of our army," the article said. The church building "has been the scene of several picket skirmishes." It had also been the scene of worship services for troops with the army chaplain.

Confederate troops seized the church a few weeks later, holding it for a month before retreating further into Virginia. The Union army controlled the church for the rest of the Civil War. First they used it as a hospital. One man recorded a visit to the church at the time. "He was fourteen, and had been sent with his sister to take some refreshments to a wounded Confederate prisoner. The officer in charge was very courteous and escorted him and his young sister to the soldier lying ill in one of the pews. The captured Confederate was given the same care as other wounded. There must have been a hundred wounded soldiers

The Falls Church historic property in the 1860s.

inside the church, two or three in each box-like pew."[3]

The Union army later tore out the floor and used the church as a stable. Many items were taken from the church, from silver pieces to the baptismal font. A few items made their way back over time. The granddaughter of a New York officer returned a communion chalice almost a century later. The government repaired the extensive damage caused by Union forces. It patched the walls and replaced the floors. It installed new windows and frames.

Still, the war had left its scars. This would not be the last time the church would serve as a stage for national division.

The church's membership ebbed and flowed in the following decades. It was as low as twenty-one communicants in the late 1800s, rising to seventy-five at the turn of the 19th century. Around that time, the rector George Summerville worked tirelessly to raise funds for more repairs. While still on a fundraising trip to New England in 1908, he died the same week that the interior restoration was completed.

In the 1930s, attendance averaged a little over 100 each Sunday. At the two hundredth anniversary of the church in 1934, the church invited luminaries such as the President of the United States and the Governor of Virginia. Franklin D. Roosevelt sent flowers for the altar with personal regrets. The governor did the same.

The church hired a new minister in 1935—Watkins Leigh Ribble. A parishioner at the time wrote this about Mr. Ribble: "the church has prospered perhaps as never before, both spiritually and materially." Over his ten years as rector, the number of communicants rose from 186 to 341, and annual giving from $4,000 to $10,000 (about $175,000 in today's dollars).

After World War II, the population of the Washington D.C. region exploded, lifting the membership of the church with it. Frances Hayes was the rector for twelve years during this period. In 1956, the year before he resigned, the church had grown to 1,261 communicants.

This increase in size prompted a building campaign. In 1959, rector Hodge Alves led the church to add a balcony that had been envisioned at the time of original construction. A ten-year building campaign, costing almost $500,000, expanded the church significantly. New buildings were added, the grounds were improved, and a custom organ was added to the historic church.

But the growth would not last. The Falls Church would soon be caught up in the sharp declines that swept across the entire Episcopal denomination.

The Episcopal Drift and Renewal

The Episcopal Church was founded in 1789, the year of the U.S. Constitution. This was no coincidence. The church, while a direct offshoot of the Church of England, shielded American clergy from the authority of the British monarchy. It remained a member of the Anglican Communion, but with its own authority and bishops. This separate-but-related structure maintained a link to the past while giving the denomination freedom to chart its own course in the future.

The historic sanctuary to the left; new buildings added in 1959 to the right.

Tradition still figured prominently in the Episcopal Church. Like its parent Anglican Communion, the church incorporated liturgy from the Book of Common Prayer. This liturgy, originating with the 16th century English Reformation, offers a spirit of traditional reverence. As a clergyman at The Falls Church put it, "The liturgy allows people to go deeper. So we don't have as many conversions, but we have many transfers. Lutherans have confirmation and great hymns, Baptists have magisterial Sunday schools, and we have liturgy."

The Episcopal Church's rich heritage has included close ties to national leadership. Many American Founders counted among the church's membership. Roughly one-fourth of all U.S. Presidents have been Episcopalians—from George Washington and James Madison to Franklin D. Roosevelt and George H.W. Bush. Wealthy families like the Vanderbilts and the Morgans were known as members. This history has lent an air of sophistication, even elitism, within the denomination.

In the mid-twentieth century, the denomination reached its peak membership of over 3.4 million. It became a leading proponent of social progress, passing a resolution in 1958 to work toward racial equality and integration and another resolution in the 1970s to support the ordination of women. These changes were not without controversy, and they were precursors of starker conflicts to come.

The turbulence within the Episcopal Church was always felt at The Falls Church, near the political heart of America. In 1966, the rector of the Falls Church, Joseph Hodge Alves, wrote these words about the swirl of the Sixties culture: a congregation "must keep a sane balance that will enable it to be a spiritual home for honest men of varying opinions. The ministry of the Church must always contain the quality of reconciliation. Worship is the heart of a congregation's life, as we have said constantly. It is in this act that we hear God's judgment on each person and the world. It is here that we together seek God's guidance in a changing and confusing day of great promise."[4]

While those words ring true, they failed to mention where Jesus Christ might fit within the "varying opinions" and "confusing day." Already the primary emphasis seemed to be turning away from Jesus, and to secondary virtues like reconciliation. Francis Long, a Falls Church member for many decades, remembers attending the annual meeting of the Virginia Diocese in 1969. She was the first-ever female delegate from The Falls Church. "That year, and probably before that," she said, "there were rumblings of things that didn't sit right." It was not yet a particular hot-button issue, but it was about the Bible as the true word of God.

Around the nation, prominent Episcopal bishops, such as James Pike of California, started questioning long-held and widely accepted Christian beliefs. Several times heresy procedures were begun, but each time the Episcopal leadership decided against pursuing the charges. Wider and wider variances of beliefs and practices grew unchecked within the church. And membership was falling.

In the mid-1970s, an Episcopal pastor named Terry Fullam called out this danger within the church: "We have lost—that is, our particular branch of the church, the Episcopal Church—we have lost one member every five minutes for ten years. There's death everywhere in the church."[5] The numbers bore this out. Between 1970 and 1990, national membership declined by nearly one million.

Amidst this decline, leaders like Terry Fullam worked for renewal. In 1972, he became the rector of Saint Paul's, a quiet and quaint Episcopal church in Darien, Connecticut. He accepted this lead pastor position only on the condition "that Christ be true head of the church." His teaching emphasized life in the Holy Spirit for everyone in the church, and his charismatic leadership sparked renewal. Saint Paul's became one of the fastest growing churches in the United States—attendance doubled in three years, and giving increased even more. The turnaround inspired a book: *Miracle in Darien* by Bob Slosser.

The Falls Church, however, was like most dwindling Episcopal churches that did not have a Terry Fullam at the helm. Joel Pugh, the church's beloved rector, had retired in 1978. With no successor in place, the church began to lose members. The church formed a search committee, which settled on a bold plan. They wanted someone young and vibrant. They wanted someone who could bring in new people. Someone like Terry Fullam.

The church assigned its senior warden—the highest-ranking non-clergy position—to lead the search. The committee was thorough, considering hundreds of applicants. This took time. Lots of time. Two years passed without a replacement and church membership continued to slip. Sundays passed with fewer than one hundred in attendance.

"Morale suffered," one member said. "We were a struggling little community, working to survive a spiritual drought, having been without a rector for too long."

That was all about to change.

3

A New Rector

Hear, my son, your father's instruction,
and forsake not your mother's teaching,
for they are a graceful garland for your head
and pendants for your neck.

Proverbs 1:8-9

John Yates was right where he wanted to be.

His early career had put his young family through many moves. He and his wife Susan, soon after graduating from the University of North Carolina at Chapel Hill, had packed up for seminary at Princeton. A few years later, youth ministry drew them to Columbia, South Carolina. Then they went to serve a church outside Pittsburgh.

Seven years, three moves, five kids. They were ready to settle down.

God had other plans.

A Man's Foundation

Great souls do not grow in a vacuum. Some manage to rise out of challenging circumstances—poverty and strife. But those are the storybook tales. The likelier successes arise in good families, where the foundations of character are built over generations of honest and faithful men and women. To show this, John Yates has told a story of two families in New England. One of the families had a praying

12

patriarch, the other didn't.

The praying patriarch was a pastor. He had at least 929 descendants. Almost half of those were ministers. Eighty-six became university professors. Thirteen became university presidents. Five were elected to the United States House of Representatives, and two to the Senate. One became Vice President of the United States. The patriarch of this family was Jonathan Edwards, a man who prayed for his family.

The other man was a contemporary of Edwards. He spent much of his life in prison. He wasn't known to be a believer; he didn't take his children to church. He had at least 1,026 descendants. Of his family, 300 went to prison for an average of thirteen years; 190 were prostitutes; and 680 were admitted alcoholics. His family served as a radical example of family dysfunction. It might have helped if this patriarch had prayed a little more.[6]

The family of John Yates was much closer to the legacy of Jonathan Edwards. They'd been strong for generations. Yates's great-great-grandfather was a preacher named William Black Yates. He was converted on the operating bed in the early 1800s. This was before anesthesia. In the midst of the pain, confronted by his own mortality, he found God and committed himself to the Lord. He soon put his commitment to action, teaching the gospel on the tough docks of Charleston, South Carolina. He led a local chapel for sailors and families. He founded an orphanage for children whose parents died during the Civil War. That legacy of faithful action passed down through the generations.

Both John and Susan Yates credit their parents and grandparents for teaching them this faith, a faith that was strengthened in Episcopal churches. "We have amazing grandmothers." John smiles at the memory of them. He calls Susan's mother "the wisest woman I have ever known." He applauds how she loved unconditionally, how she gave without holding back. As for his own mother, John does not shy away from her pivotal role in his faith. "I caught my love of the word of God from my mother, who patiently read to me the Bible stories every night at bedtime and talked with me about them, helping me learn and understand scripture." Today John and Susan have her portrait hanging above the fireplace mantle in the family living room.

From those roots, John developed a deep well of faith. But he still had his season of questions. He took religion classes in college. As he put it, he hoped "rather naively to strengthen my trust in God, but after four or five classes in Old Testament and New Testament, I wondered if I could honestly believe what I read in the Bible." Doubts arose from the way the Scriptures were taught. John began to question the biblical faith that his parents and his home church had planted in his heart.

At the same time, he found rich community with fellow believers in a national youth ministry, Young Life. He also met Peter Moore, who had founded a ministry for leading East Coast schools. "Peter was the first minister I had ever met who was so sharp and so full of vision for renewing the Episcopal denomination. He had a huge impact on me. He introduced me to Jim Packer in 1965. He introduced me to John Stott. These turned out to be formative connections."

Yates assumed his path was clear after college. Like most young men, he expected to be drafted and shipped out for Vietnam. But it was not to be. Because of a minor physical infirmity, he was disqualified from the draft. That left him with little time to figure out what came next. He believed deep down that God was most important, but he had a lot of questions about his faith. He wanted to be sure with his head what he believed in his heart—to figure out what he believed about the Bible and about the Holy Spirit. Nothing could accomplish this better than time immersed in the Scriptures. John applied and was accepted to Princeton seminary. While there, under great teachers, he studied and wrestled with his questions and came to a conclusion: "the Scriptures are indeed true."

That settled John's biggest question, but it did not tell him what to do with his life. He and Susan had married soon after college and were living in Princeton when they caught a vision of God's plan. While attending a conference, they met with Susan's godfather, the missionary bishop to Alaska in the Episcopal Church. He had been Susan's father's roommate throughout college, and he had served in John's hometown church in North Carolina. He had connections to them both, and he took them aside and gave them a simple message that they would never forget: "I know you've been involved with Campus Crusade and Young Life, and these are wonderful ministries, but we really need young people like you in the church. We need what you've got to help people in the church come alive to Christ. Would you consider joining me in trying to bring about renewal in the Episcopal Church?"

John and Susan heard a call in these words. Over the next year they prayed about it, and they decided God was leading them to work for change within the church. John finished seminary and took a job in youth ministry at a church in South Carolina.

After a few years there, in the early 1970s, John accepted a new position in an Episcopal church called St. Stephens in Sewickly, Pennsylvania. He became the associate rector, focusing on ministry to young families under the lead rector, John Guest.

"John Guest came from England to the United States with a guitar on his back," John said. "He had the gift of evangelism and leadership. I learned from him how to turn a church around." John Guest transformed the sleepy, little traditional church in Sewickly into an alive, exciting, evangelistic church with a huge impact in Pennsylvania—much as St. Paul's had been renewed under Terry Fullam's leadership in Connecticut. Yates loved working with John Guest, and he learned much from him.

Yates also found a powerful example right in his own neighborhood: Bishop Alfred Stanway. The bishop, known as Alf, had lived an impressive life and had retired to his home country of Australia. He came out of retirement to lead a new seminary in Pennsylvania—Trinity School for Ministry. When he made the move, he ended up living across the street from the Yates family.

"He had a titanic impact on me," John said. "Not many people get pictures in my office. Alf does." The framed picture sat on John's bookshelf, showing a stately, wise-looking bishop. "Alf Stanway had the gifts of leadership, administration, and faith." He also modeled daily discipline. "Every morning, the light came on in Alf's study about 5:30. I knew, as I looked across the darkened way, that that old man was studying scripture and praying. I wanted with all my heart to be like him."

The years in Pennsylvania were good to the Yates family. John had these great men to learn from. He and Susan were building community and growing in their walk with the Lord. They were even expecting twins—their fourth and fifth children.

Other churches were interested in hiring John as a lead pastor, but he was not answering their calls. He had no reason to leave.

Following God's Call

"I had the best father-in-law," John said. "He never told me what to do."

That's what made it so exceptional when Susan's father gave John some advice in early 1979. He knew about churches having interest in John. He knew about John not taking their calls. So he asked John a question: "If you never talk to these people, how do you know you won't miss God's call?"

John had to admit it was a good point. Little did he know that around the same time, a historic church in northern Virginia was not doing well and had an interest in a new rector. More than anything, the church had an interest in John Yates.

The Falls Church search committee made its first call to Yates in April 1979. They wanted to visit his church in Pennsylvania to hear him preach. They came the Sunday after the Yates's twins were born. John was preaching, and he had two newborns. He did not have much interest in these visitors.

But they were impressed with what they saw. They invited John to visit the church in Virginia. Heeding the words from his father-in-law, John took up their invitation.

Frances Long attended the Falls Church at the time. She remembers John's first visit clearly. "One Sunday we noticed when two blond-haired men, definitely young men, showed up at the church." They stood out among the gray hair in the pews. One of those men was Yates, visiting the church for the first time. He'd brought a friend who could help him assess the place.

On the trip back to Pennsylvania, Yates thought, "Gee, they need somebody just like you, John." He paused. "I wonder who they're going to get."

He still wasn't convinced he was the one, even though he recognized the fit. He returned home to Susan, his ten-day-old twins, and three other young children.

The Falls Church made a strong next move. They sent John a telegram the following day. The message said that the search committee believed, unanimously, that God had appointed him to be the church's rector. It added that the church would wait until God made that clear for him.

John and Susan didn't like the idea. They didn't want to leave, but they didn't know what to do about this message. "We would have loved to have stayed in Pittsburgh all of our lives," John said. "But we began to realize that God was doing something, and we had to agree with it. I remember the time when Susan and I finally got honest with each other, and we both admitted to one another that we believed God wanted us to come to Virginia. We were both so sad about it that we cried in each other's arms, standing in the living room there in Pittsburgh."

They decided it would be best if they left quickly, because it wasn't going to be easy. And so John, Susan, and the five kids moved to Fall Church, Virginia, in July 1979.

A Leader's Vision

Imagine a giant, frozen ocean. The sky is immense and slate gray. Snow is falling, piling up on the ice. There's no land—no variation—as far as you can see.

Now, in the midst of that ocean sits a large ship. It sought the North Pole, but the water froze around it. Now it's stuck. A few people are on board. Their food is running low. But somehow a new captain shows up.

What should he do?

That's the image Yates saw when he became the rector of the Falls Church in the summer of 1979. He took on the role of captain, and thanks to his training in Pennsylvania and his mentors, he had an idea about what to do. He needed to build fires around the ship's perimeter. He had to help kindle the fire of the spirit and get that ship turned around. He also didn't want to lose anybody if he could avoid it.

This was far from easy. "I was 32 when I came," John said. "The church was 250, and most members were over 50. I came in with energy and evangelism." The age difference was so significant that one Sunday, as John greeted church-goers at the door, a woman mistook him for a youthful Acolyte.

John's predecessor, Joel Pugh, was scholarly, grey-haired, and dignified. "I was none of that," John said with a laugh. "And I brought in men like John Stott who spoke unabashedly about changing the Episcopal Church."

While John and Susan Yates tried to change very little about the church in their first year, their presence immediately left a mark. They brought five children. They brought a youthful, energetic spirit—to a church that had 24 funerals in that first year. They also pushed to get Bibles in the pews, instead of only the Book of Common Prayer. Even this faced opposition in the church.

The Yates family in 1979. John, Susan,
Allison, Chris, John, Libby, and Susy.

The challenges John faced were, in many ways, previews of what was to come. Some already saw trouble ahead. The year that he came to the historic Falls Church also happened to be the year that the Episcopal Church passed a resolution regarding church property. The Episcopal Church has a General Convention every three years, where the church makes important decisions. At the 1979 General Convention, one resolution pronounced that all church property would be owned by the Episcopal Church, not the local congregation. Few paid much attention to it at the time. Yates had no idea about it. That would change decades later.

Two other notable things happened in the Episcopal Church in 1979. First, Bishop Edmond Browning publicly declared that he would "not obey or enforce the church's official traditional teaching on sexuality." Five years later, Browning would become the Presiding

Bishop—the leader of the Episcopal Church. Second, John Shelby "Jack" Spong became an Episcopal bishop in New Jersey. Like Yates, Jack Spong had attended the University of North Carolina at Chapel Hill. He had even worked with Susan Yates's father. But his views on faith were changing, diverging from tradition, and his influence was growing.

The seeds of tension were planted. It was a story of new versus old, of liberal versus evangelical, but more than anything, of what faith meant.

Yates was in the thick of it. He was lighting fires, and the ice was thawing. He was also keeping people on the ship as well as he could. But, with all this change, he couldn't keep the boat from rocking.

4

The Boat Rocked

The Church exists for nothing else but
to draw men into Christ, to make them little Christs.
If they are not doing that, all the cathedrals, clergy, missions, sermons, even the
Bible itself, are simply a waste of time.
C.S. Lewis, *Mere Christianity*

"Why is he preaching about Jesus so much?"

That was the question on many long-timers' minds. It wasn't that people at The Falls Church didn't care about faith, but focusing too much on Jesus could make people uncomfortable. The Episcopal Church was supposed to be a comfortable place. And The Falls Church, in particular, was a stately place, with a colonial brick building and a legacy going back to George Washington. It was uncouth to be fired up for Christ. It also left out many interesting topics, like church missions and education and charity.

None of these concerns altered John Yates's focus. As his wife Susan explains, "Our prayer when we came to the church was that it would be built on Jesus, not on John Yates." John and Susan understood the danger of churches centered on a single personality. "It's Biblical," Susan says. "Everyone is fallible, broken."

This recognition meant doing some unusual things within the Episcopal Church, such as regularly inviting other, strong pastors to speak on Sunday mornings. Many have preached at The Falls Church over the years, from Anglican Archbishops to the chaplain of the U.S.

21

Senate.

Still, Yates regularly used the rector's primary advantage: the pulpit. He was the only one who, week after week, could rise up before the congregation and talk to them, uninterrupted, for half an hour. This would have a profound and lasting impact.

First Impressions

Martha Cole remembers Yates's first sermon at The Falls Church. She'd started attending the church on and off in 1978, a year before he arrived. The church was in her neighborhood. She'd bring her six kids with her.

"No one spoke to us," she said of the months before his arrival. "It was full of gray hairs. It wasn't very alive, but a group of them had been praying for change."

The change showed up in a hurry with that first sermon by Yates. "I knew immediately," Martha said, "this was a preacher right in the Word."

She smiled, searching for the right words. "It was clear John had the Holy Spirit. I just knew. I felt it. My kids sensed it, too. The six of them were in grade school or younger. When John preached, the kids were enthralled. They didn't play around or fidget in the pews. They listened to his sermons. We always talked about them together."

Martha's kids even started repeating things from the sermons at home. "John had a stronger North Carolina drawl back then," Martha said. "He'd talk about *setting hearts on fire*—like, on fiiirre. Well, then my kids would go around the house saying, *on fiiire!*"

After hearing John's first sermon, Martha started coming every Sunday. She, like many others, felt that the early sermons were spoken directly to her, and she's been listening to John preach ever since.

A sermon in the summer of 1980 shows a little of what Martha Cole meant about Yates having the Holy Spirit. Envision him leaning forward on the lectern, hands folded, like he's sitting across the table from you in the dining room. His theme was the fruits of the Spirit:

> The first thing that happens when a person opens his life to Christ in faith is that he receives the Holy Spirit; the actual Spirit of God himself comes to dwell within him. The Holy Spirit begins to do a miracle inside our life, as gradually and slowly and surely as we let Him. ... [This] helps us put to death the old nature and live the new life. But, we never totally achieve it; there is always a struggle in the Christian life, and we should understand that and accept that. *God is not looking for perfect people, he's looking for progressing people who are honest about their own shortcomings.*

Yates went on to describe how important fruit—edible fruit—was in Jewish culture in Bible times. He quoted Jesus's words on being the true vine, and on pruning. He painted a metaphor of a garden. Then, with the congregation's complete and undivided attention, he fixed his warm and welcoming eyes on the crowd.

> There's no better garden atmosphere than the atmosphere of the local church. For you and I, dear people, are made for growth. We're not made to stay on the same level. We are made for fruitfulness. Not necessarily to become just more religious and participate in religious activities, but to become better and better. You know, full ripe fruit is irresistible, and a church full of people who are growing and producing the fruit of the Spirit is irresistible to the people around.[7]

As time would show, The Falls Church would become just such a place.

Too Much Spirit for Some

At an early vestry retreat, the challenges facing Yates took clear form. A well-groomed, old-school Virginia woman—a *true* Episcopalian woman—stared Yates straight in the eyes.

"I don't like you," she said.

She and others wanted Yates to change, to be more like other Episcopal rectors.

Not long after that, the junior warden—the church's second-ranking lay leader—sent Yates his resignation letter. While Yates was far from excited about keeping onboard someone who didn't want to work with him, he didn't accept the resignation. He asked the junior warden to finish his term. The man did that, and then he left. He took some of the congregation with him.

This division was not what Yates wanted. He formed a committee of four within the vestry—the eighteen lay leaders of the church who had been there when he arrived. He picked two people on his side and two people against him. The committee met regularly. They talked through the issues, and it helped. Much of the disagreement arose from style and misunderstanding. These committee meetings helped reassure the church's old guard.

Charlie Powell was one of Yates's close friends and confidants in those days. "It was hard on him," Charlie remembers. "We would walk and talk and pray. We didn't get into specifics, but I think I was an encouragement to him. Johnny didn't have many like-minded men his age in the church at first. Some of the old guard didn't like his leadership. They were uncomfortable."

Yates's first hire helped with this challenge. He thought they should hire a youth minister. The vestry disagreed. They wanted someone older, someone who could handle the needs of the older church through pastoral care.

The vestry's suggestion made sense: the church had no youth. But Yates said, "That's why we a need a youth minister!"

The vestry denied Yates's request. In the meantime, he met an older clergyman, John Parke, at a conference. Parke had an ability to relate to and pastor the older congregation at that time. So the church brought on Parke—thirty years Yates's senior—to be the associate rector.

"He was wonderful," Yates said. "He was even more radical than I was!" By "radical," Yates had in mind the intensity of devotion to what mattered most. He would make sure that no one in the pews had any doubt about what the most important thing was.

Preaching on Just One Thing

On July 20, 1980, about a year after he'd arrived, as discontentment simmered, Yates preached on Luke's story of Jesus's visit with Mary and Martha soon before He died. "It's one of the best stories in all the Bible," Yates said. He described how Martha busied herself with preparing an elaborate meal for Jesus, while Mary just sat at the Lord's feet and listened to his teaching.

> If there are two words that describe the predicament of modern America, they could not be better chosen than these— 'commotion' in our 'divided minds.' We are so incredibly busy—we are carrying in our minds so many ideas, obligations and concerns that sometimes it seems as though a noisy traffic jam is going on inside our soul!
>
> Jesus said to Martha, 'Martha, just one thing is necessary'— just a sandwich will be plenty—one course is enough. Slow down, forget your elaborate preparation. Mary has chosen the best thing—join us.
>
> Just one thing is enough. This is a word we need to hear today.

Yates's message continued building toward the key insight for the church. He told a story to make crystal clear to that congregation— including many successful business leaders—that just one thing was enough, and that the one thing was Jesus:

> Many years ago, the president of Bethlehem Steel called in a consultant and asked him to help him increase the company's productivity and said that he would pay whatever the advice

was worth. The consultant gave him one simple guideline, 'when you first arrive at your office in the morning, decide on the single most important thing which you must accomplish that day. Put everything else aside and just attack that one project. Try this for a few months and send me a check for whatever you think the advice is worth.' Two, three months went by and one day the consultant received in the mail a check for $25,000. The executive had shared the advice with his assistants and as they seriously sought to follow it, the benefits were immediate and obvious. *Just one thing at a time is enough.*

You, perhaps, are saying, 'Well you don't know what it is like in my office or in my home, things are simply too busy and complicated to do just one thing at a time.' But the principle is true – just one thing is enough for any one time. We are tyrannized by the urgent.

Jesus, of course, was talking about *The One Thing* that is most important in all of life. He was not just talking about the material things such as preparation for dinner parties or office work. He was talking about the spiritual side of life. The most important thing in all of life is knowing the Lord. Whoever you are, whatever you do, nothing you do is as important as the time you spend in deepening the quality of your relationship with the Lord. 'Mary has chosen the good portion which shall not be taken away from her.' You or I may lose everything – eyesight, job, home, savings, your friends, your family. But no one can take away from you your relationship with God.[8]

A few months after that sermon, the country was swept up in a time of change—election season in the days before Ronald Reagan became President. Yates knew how political turmoil could affect the church members in the Washington area. "All of us this week are more aware of being a part of a time of great change. Our president is being replaced by a vastly different man. Our Senate is changing and the whole direction of political attitudes seems to be shifting."

He preached about the many other changes underway. "This is an age of impermanence," he said. "We long for a sense of security and a rock on which to stand."

Then he took the congregation with him to a personal place. "Sometimes when I am longing for things to stop for a while, and remain the same, I'm drawn to my home; I want to go back to the old farm, Tothill, down in North Carolina. That place seems more permanent in my mind, but even there, where I grew up and shared so many happy hours with my family as a boy, things are changing. The old horses are now gone, the old cattle have been replaced, the large trees are dying and being replaced by younger ones."

All of this set up Yates's return to his singular focus:

> Everything changes—everything, that is, except God. For God, history is but the unfolding of His story, and behind all things He remains the same. This theme rings through both the Old Testament and the New Testament. To the Hebrews who were struggling to rebuild a nation after the Babylonian captivity, the prophet Malachi spoke forth God's word and he said, "For I the Lord do not change."

> Toward the end of the First Century the young church was being shaken to the core by violent persecution, desertion and by heretical teaching. During these discouraging days of displacement the writers to the Hebrews wrote these words of encouragement to the exhausted young church: "Fix your eyes on Jesus the author and perfector of your faith. Jesus Christ is the same—yesterday, and today, and yes, forever."

Yates encouraged the church to hold fast to this truth in any condition. "God is the same, Christ is the same, and so too finally, our mission must be the same in the midst of confusing times. We are continually to love God, to love one another, and to proclaim this unchanging Lord Jesus Christ to our generation."[9]

This mission was beginning to awaken the church. New people were joining, and they would need to grow together, to unite around the unchanging Christ, because turbulent times lay ahead.

5

The People Came

Jesus came and said to them, "All authority in heaven and on earth
has been given to me. Go therefore and make disciples of all nations,
baptizing them in the name of the Father and of the Son and of the Holy Spirit,
teaching them to observe all that I have commanded you.
And behold, I am with you always, to the end of the age."
Matthew 28:18-20

Churches don't grow overnight from a hundred or so people to several thousand. The Lord was at work, but there were no lightning strikes. Growing something important takes time. Membership requires commitment, down to the soul. The modern era could learn something from the patient building that happened in the early 1980s at The Falls Church.[10]

Green Shoots

Never underestimate the power of a simple invitation. Howard Shafferman met John and Susan Yates at a wedding in the summer of 1979. They hit it off. "We're going to be leading a church in Falls Church," Susan said. "You should come!"

So Howard did. He joined the church in September 1979. "Aside from the Yates, there were only a few young people in the church then. I was one of them. Another was Susan's cousin." Howard didn't let it stay that way for long. He saw that The Falls Church was becoming a special place. He invited friends who, like him, had graduated from law school the year before. Many visited, and those who did stayed. The cadre of young members grew.

But not everyone was eager to try an Episcopal church. Later that fall, Charlie Powell, a recent seminary graduate from the West Coast, was looking for the right church fit in the area. He and his wife Esther had just moved from Portland, Oregon. One night they attended a debut showing of *The Jesus Film* at the Kennedy Center. At intermission, Charlie and his wife rose for a break. Three rows behind them were two familiar faces. They had met John and Susan Yates before in organizations like Campus Crusade, but it had been years since they had seen each other. The two couples struck up an easy conversation.

It wasn't long before Susan said, "You don't have a home church here yet. Come and see what we're doing."

"Of course!" said Esther.

Charlie figured they would go once. He liked John and Susan, but in the back of his mind, he had doubts. His degree was from a conservative Baptist seminary. The Episcopal denomination had little of the Baptist fire in it. Charlie wondered, "What would my professors and friends from school think?"

His wife Esther kept pressing him, and they visited The Falls Church a few months later, in the spring of 1980. It was the Sunday when Yates interviewed the first graduates of the church's new member class. Charlie was struck by the honest discussions of their faith.

"I thought, *Wow, what an impressive group.*" Charlie paused. "It was very compelling. It was evidence of the early work of the Spirit in that place. Anyone could show up in that church for a first visit, and even if they sat in the back row, they'd feel it. There's a pastoral affability that Johnny exudes. He and Susan made the whole place feel like family."

After the Powell's first visit, it didn't take much convincing for Charlie to come again. "The more we were there," he said, "the more we got involved."

Ten years later, Charlie found himself on staff and counted John as one of his best friends.

Many new visitors to The Falls Church recounted similar experiences in those early months. The congregation grew dramatically. It was no accident, and it was just the beginning. A focus on evangelism propelled the growth.

In August 1980, Yates preached to the 250 or so members about the importance of work that lasts forever. Two types of that work are loving people and bringing others to Christ. On the second type, Yates said:

> I don't know how many citizens of Heaven will be there because of my life and witness. I know that I will only be there because of the life and witness of my parents who shared with me the Good News of the Gospel. But I hope there will be thousands of people there because of my life. Now, listen, I'm not an evangelist. I don't have the gift of evangelism that's described in the Bible. I'm simply a witness for Christ. There are not many evangelists in the church. I'd be happy if one out of 25 people in the church were an evangelist. But one need not have the gift of evangelism to show to others the way to Heaven. You and I are presenting Christianity and Christ to the persons around us every day. Is it the kind of Christianity that will cause other people to want to come to know God? Is it the kind of Christianity that would cause others to hunger for a closer relationship with God?

Yates went on to explain that no one, alone, is adequate. But together they are. "There's a story of an interview in Heaven. It occurred shortly after Jesus returned to Heaven, and He was talking to an angel.

'What is your method,' the angel asked, 'for proclaiming the message to all the world?'

Jesus said, 'I have entrusted it to a few humble men and women.'

'And if they fail?'

'I have no other plan,' was Jesus's reply."

Yates met the eyes in the congregation. He drew them closer, as if he spoke to each person directly. His voice grew softer. "*We* are His plan for leading people into eternal life. The Christian's work, whatever his vocation, must be by loving deeds and careful witness to bring other people to faith in Jesus Christ. This is not an option. These are our marching orders."[11]

The Spreading Word

Sam and Judy Thomsen were living in Botswana when they first heard about The Falls Church. They had spent much of the 1970s in Africa on a tour of duty with the U.S. Foreign Service. They had become friends with the Bishop of Botswana. When they were due to return to Washington, D.C., the Bishop encouraged them to meet a bright, young pastor named John Yates. They visited The Falls Church once and found their new home. It was a church that fed them and their family of teenage kids.

If news had reached Botswana, it was certainly spreading around America's capital.

Mark and Katherine Weller came from different church backgrounds. She was a long-time Episcopalian. He grew up Presbyterian and wasn't a big fan of liturgy. They moved to Washington from Indiana as a young married couple in 1983. They were visiting a few churches but hadn't found the right fit.

Mark worked in the Senate and had a Bible study with a few other young staffers. Eventually he asked the chaplain of the Senate, Dick Halvorson, if he had any church recommendations. Dick knew the area well. Before becoming the chaplain, he'd served for years as the senior pastor at a Presbyterian church in Bethesda.

"There's only one place to go," Dick told Mark. "The Falls

Church. They have a great young pastor, John Yates."

Mark and Katherine visited on Palm Sunday. "We immediately felt it was the place for us," Katherine said. But the church didn't leave ministry to chance. When Mark and Katherine attended that first day, they filled out a visitor card. The very next week people from the church came to their apartment and shared about their faith.

This was evangelism explosion, or "EE" in action. The program was another part of how The Falls Church equipped its members. Mark and Katherine got involved.

Word about The Falls Church was also spreading in other Episcopal circles.

Julia Mitchell grew up in the Episcopal Church and went to an Episcopal all-girls school. In the mid-1980s, she was attending an Episcopal church in nearby Old Town Alexandria. But some friends told her about a different kind of Episcopal church.

Julia went to The Falls Church for the first time with two kids under three—and no husband, as she had recently divorced. The kids sat on her lap. "All it took was that service," she said. "I found my home. It felt like a place where I wanted to raise my kids."

Julia noticed things that were special about The Falls Church. "John's preaching was so straightforward, so clear, speaking from the heart," she said. "It wasn't 'preachy.' It was fresh and genuine." Julia also noticed that other men in the church were engaged. Julia saw how they became connected and held each other accountable. She thought, "If the men are getting fed, then families are getting fed, and so women must be getting fed." As Julia had guessed, the women were wonderful to her. She was working and had real needs as a single mother, and the church helped meet those needs. Many women embraced her and her family. A tone of deep gratitude and joy touched her voice as she said, "They helped me raise my kids."

Like Julia, Frank and Virginia Watson were also long-time Episcopalians. They had been attending the same Episcopal church in northern Virginia for twenty years. But Frank Watson was growing uncomfortable with the teaching, as it was moving away from orthodoxy. Virginia remembers sitting beside Frank during services. "I could feel him getting tight beside me, tensing up at the preacher's sermon."

They were hesitant to leave the church they'd attended for two decades, and their strong community there. But The Falls Church tugged at them. They'd met Yates through Episcopal Diocese meetings. In January 1989, they decided to visit.

"We went that first Sunday and never tried another church." Virginia tried to downplay this decision to leave her prior church. "I'm not the type to rattle the cage," she said. "I don't like church hopping." She still had many friends at their old church who, she thinks, simply chose to ignore what the Episcopal leadership was doing.

Jean and Al Trakowski have a similar story. They'd been going to another nearby Episcopal church. Jean Trakowski had been there 21 years. "We liked it, but the rector, while great at pastoral care, was a terrible preacher. If we didn't find another church," Jean flashed a joking smile, then continued in her polished British accent, "I fear Al would have fallen out of the faith."

So Al and Jean asked the rector at their church if he recommended any other places. The rector pointed them to The Falls Church.

The Trakowskis visited three weeks after the Yates family arrived. As with almost everyone else, it took just one visit for Al and Jean to know that The Falls Church was home. They stayed for 35 years.

But not everyone fell in love with the church at first sight. Dan and Jackie Henneberg had moved to Northern Virginia in 1970. They searched for a good church. They tried all kinds, but never found one that was home. While they settled on an established Episcopal church in the area, it was not satisfying.

"There were good people there," Dan said. "The church was like a social club. We had friends and we enjoyed it. But there was no spirit." Jackie had grown up Baptist, so like Charlie Powell, she didn't take much to the sleepy denomination.

Fast-forward ten years, to 1980. Someone told the Hennebergs about a new pastor at The Falls Church. They went to check it out. But on their first visit, John Yates was out of town. Dan recalled, "It seemed like any other Episcopal church. Nothing special." And he knew, because he'd grown up Episcopalian.

Six months later, they decided to revisit The Falls Church. Again Yates was out of town, but this time he had invited a bishop from South America to preach. "He had the gospel," Dan remembered. "We felt something special might be going on, so we decided to keep visiting."

The next time the Hennebergs came, Yates was preaching. "We just knew," Dan said, thinking back to the sermon that day. "He had a rare gift of preaching. The Spirit was in that place. The Holy Spirit was working through John and Susan." Like most people, Dan couldn't quite put his finger on it. "You could just *feel* it," he said. "But I really noticed it because we were still going back and forth with our old church. We had commitments to finish there. The contrast between the two places was stark. One had the life of the Spirit in it, the other didn't."

Meeting People Where They Are

A common thread to all these newcomers at The Falls Church was a deep resonance with John Yates's preaching. "He was speaking right to me," one would say. Another: "I felt like he said exactly what I needed to hear."

Yates's sermons from those early years help show why people felt this way. If a topic was in the media, it was on people's minds, and Yates gave them a framework for understanding it as Jesus would, according to Jesus' teaching.

One of the biggest events of 1981 was the attempted assassination of President Ronald Reagan. On March 30, sixty-nine days into his presidency, Reagan walked out of the Washington Hilton Hotel waving to a crowd of reporters and others. Only thirty feet separated him from his limousine. Secret Service agents surrounded him, but a group of unscreened people stood close as the President walked by. One of the men, fifteen feet away, was John Hinckley.

Hinckley opened fire with a handgun. He unloaded six shots in two seconds.

One of the bullets hit President Reagan's left arm and penetrated his chest. As the Secret Service rushed the President to medical care, he coughed up blood.

Doctors at George Washington Hospital rushed President Reagan into surgery. He lost over half of his blood in the emergency room and during surgery. The operation was a success, removing the bullet that had lodged an inch from his heart. Reagan stayed in the hospital two weeks.

The assassination attempt was felt throughout America. The U.S. Senate adjourned. The Academy Awards were postponed. Stocks fell, the New York Stock Exchange closed early. And the following Sunday, Yates addressed one of the hardest questions of the Christian faith: *If God Is A Good God, Why Tragedy?*

You and I live in a world where all is not right. Mankind and even the natural world itself have been affected by man's sin in ways we do not even begin to understand yet. Until history is brought to a climax and Satan is destroyed forever by God, there will be sadness, tragedy, and heartaches, even for those who seek to obey God.

But we must never forget that, in spite of all these things God's ultimate will and plans will not be thwarted. Man's sin, his carelessness and natural capriciousness, may, for a time, seem to thwart God's perfect will and His best for us, as children may temporarily dam up and divert the course of a mountain stream, but ultimately, God's will is going to be done just as the water from the stream will ultimately work its way around the children's little dam and find its way to the valley.

There are definite boundaries to man's freedom, and there is no one and no thing which can prevent God's will. His purposes will be accomplished.

Yates recognized that sounded good in theory, but that people still faced the challenge of how to live in response to difficult and tragic events. He kept to the theme a few weeks later, after the wife of the associate rector passed away. Yates preached a sermon titled, *Can Any Be Certain of Life After Death?*

Whenever a believer dies, that person simply moves into a closer relationship with God. Death is like a horizon. We cannot see beyond it from this side, but we can know that all that we have thus far experienced of life is only a momentary prelude to what God has for us on the other side. The colors, the music, the joy, and unspeakable loveliness of life with Christ in Heaven are so far beyond any of our present comprehensions. Life there will not, I think, be static. There will be excitement and purpose and growth in the life beyond. Our eyes have not seen nor our ears heard anything that can begin to be compared to the glory that Christ will reveal to his children in the greater life.

The Spirit flowed through Yates's preaching. He met people where they were, and the people continued to come. But growth presented challenges. Would the church hold fast to its values and its focus as it awakened? An answer could be found in its leader.

6

A Wise Example

People have an idea that the preacher is an actor on a stage and they are the critics, blaming or praising him. What they don't know is that they are the actors on the stage; he (the preacher) is merely the prompter standing in the wings, reminding them of their lost lines.

Søren Kierkegaard

If you want to know a man, *really* know who he is, talk to the person closest to him. Ask that person what he does when he rises in the morning. What is his first priority?

Here's Susan Yates's answer to that question about John Yates. "Ever since the beginning, ever since I've known him, he's always been faithful in getting up early and spending time on his knees, praying for me and the kids and in God's word. That has given me a real sense of security. His faith gives me security."

Yates's son, John, remembers this well. "One of my earliest childhood memories is waking early, at 6 o'clock, and sneaking downstairs. I would be on my way to the basement to watch a cartoon. The house would be dark, except that in dad's study, the light would be on. I looked in, and there would be dad, in his chair, praying, with the Bible and prayer notebook open. We would say hello, and he would go back to his prayers and I would go watch the Fantastic Four."

"Without fail, every day," added Allison, Yates's daughter. "I would wake up and smell the coffee, so I'd know dad was up. When I was little, I would go to him and snuggle in his lap. He'd tell me he was praying for me and others."

Yates followed strong examples in establishing this priority. "All my heroes were men of prayer," he said. "John Stott, Alf Stanway, Peter Moore, Chuck Miller. They were all committed to the Word of God and to prayer. I wanted to be like those men who touched my life, and I learned early on, it was essential for me to be drawn into the power of God every day."

This consistent, daily habit of prayer produced many fruits in Yates's life, especially wisdom and humility. "He's like a living book of Proverbs," said Sam Ferguson, a young pastor at The Falls Church. "It's simple, really. He spends time on his knees, and he knows the Lord. Whether it's managing time, counseling, preaching, or leading, John Yates does it with wisdom."

"He puts the word *little* before everything." Sam laughed. "John and Susan have a *little* place in the country. They go to *little* conferences and give *little* talks. This isn't false humility. It's John's consistent outward-looking approach. He's not focused on himself."

These words reflect another aspect of Yates's faith—he never shies away from drawing on the help of others. As Susan explains: "He knows his strengths and weaknesses, and he is a team leader. He seeks counsel from the people around him. He knows that he doesn't know it all. He surrounds himself with people who have gifts that he doesn't have. And that's just a biblical principle of how we are supposed to fill in the gaps for each other. John has a natural spirit of humility."

Nicholas Lubelfeld, who has worked at Yates's side for two decades as an associate rector, puts this point in his uniquely incisive words. "John is a big, roomy guy. The atmosphere around him is gracious and attractive. He is prayerfully temperate. I've been in hundreds of meetings with him over the years. I've *never* heard him shout, lay into someone, or curse or use the Lord's name in vain. He's a gentleman. He has this, *aw shucks*, Tarheel style." The impact of

John's "big, roomy" approach was clear to Nicholas. "John attracts leaders. It is congenial to be around people like yourself. A church cannot rise above the spiritual level of its leader. He is the father of the church family. He sets the tone. And here, once people come, they stay."

Yates also goes on a prayer retreat every year. He began this habit over twenty years ago, after reading of another pastor who did it. Before he leaves, he asks the parishioners to send him a card with their needs and concerns. Then, on a Sunday afternoon in August, he slips away to his farm in the country and stays through Thursday or Friday.

The week is far from restful. "For years I fasted completely," he said, "only drinking water or diluted fruit juice. In the last few years I found that my system worked better if early in the morning I ate a hard-boiled egg or a small bowl of oatmeal, but then nothing else the rest of the day. This disciplines me to focus on prayer and to remember that that is why I am there. I am always completely alone and keep outside communications at an absolute minimum."

In the early years, Yates would write a note back to each person. As the prayers requests rose well into the hundreds, this became too much. Now his assistant addresses envelopes to each person who has sent a request, including a brief, general letter from him. Then, while on his retreat, Yates reads what each person has written, and he intercedes for them. "I ask God to meet the needs in your life. It's a great privilege. It's a holy time. It's also exhausting. In some ways, it's my hardest week. It's a time of spiritual battle. Prayer is a great work."

After Yates prays for a person, he adds a short note inside the already prepared letter and puts it in the addressed envelope for mailing. "I'm grateful when I come to that last letter, and I can rest for a while."

It is easy to imagine the benefits of this retreat. Practically, it helps Yates know the needs of the people, starting at an individual level. His finger is on the pulse of the congregation, sensing where they struggle, where the church can help. "The letters people have written me through the years have contained some of the most personal, revealing, tender, and encouraging messages that this pastor has ever received. This is a huge privilege and I would not think of giving up the practice. I recommend it to every pastor."

In addition to what Yates learns during this retreat, his prayers can have a great impact. "A church moves forward on its knees," he says, and he sets the example. He ministers to the people where they need it.

One church member recalls a card that she sent. "Two years in a row, I had asked for John's prayers. I'd been estranged from one of my sons, and I'd asked for his prayers to help me find a way to enable a reconciliation. After five years . . . it's worked." She pauses, tears filling her eyes. "John had a lot to do with that. John's prayers."

Marriage and Family

Good families start with good marriages. The Yates have long championed this, and have shown the way. John and Susan—like every husband and wife—have their differences, but they make a dynamic team. John is thoughtful, wise, and slow in making decisions. Susan is quick, decisive, and visionary. Their daughter Allison summed it up: "He's a steady burning ember, she's a firecracker."

Over the years, in many sermons and talks at national conferences, John and Susan have encouraged people in marriage. "In marriage you are pushed and pressed and squeezed like in no other relationship," John said. "It pushes you to God. So marriage has been a major part of our personal discipleship. We are grateful for that. We've grown in our relationship with God because of the pressures of our life together. You don't have to be married to be a mature Christian, but that's how he worked in our lives."

The Yates's focus is on preventive medicine with honest recognitions of imperfections. "Marriage takes hard work," Susan said. "One of the most important things is forgiveness. I'm a sinful person married to a sinful person, and our selfishness just comes out. I have to ask my husband for forgiveness, but I never *feel* like doing that."

John and Susan not only modeled Christian marriage, they modeled raising a family. When they first came to the church, they had five kids under the age of seven. Their family practically doubled the number of the children in Sunday school. This meant they did not have many peers. They had moved from Pittsburgh and were, in many ways, without a community of other young parents. But the Yates's teaching and example became a strong draw for parents.

They have authored several books on the subject, including *And Then I Had Kids* and *Raising Kids With Character.* The focus of the books is practical, offering advice and guidance on the daily challenges of parenting in a complex world. And their lessons apply to any parent. "I'm often asked," Susan said, "what's it like to raise preacher's kids? One important thing is to be real. People sometimes try to put us on a pedestal, but that's false. I'm no different than the young mom sitting in the pew, and Johnny is no different than the young man who goes to work on Capitol Hill in the day. We have raised our kids to behave a certain way because Jesus is Lord, not because of their dad's profession. If Johnny were a plumber or film producer, we would raise our kids the same way."

John's focus on families became clear during his first years at the church. "In those early days," Katherine Weller explained, "so many sermons were about building strong families. This was more than just a traditional family. It was about the faith component." She thought back for a moment. "John's teaching hit right where we were in life. Sunday after Sunday, Mark and I would be on our way home and say to each other, *he was speaking to me.*"

Within his first year, John addressed parents directly:

A loving parent must be a disciplinarian. If a father or a mother simply lets a child do what he likes, and have nothing but an easy way, this would not be a truly loving parent. In fact, the Bible says here that the parent who does not discipline his child shows that he regards his child no better than an

42

illegitimate child towards whom he feels no responsibility at all.

I am concerned about the great lack of firm, loving and consistent discipline by which Christian parents raise their children. I'm concerned because I don't often see that kind of discipline. The word of God stresses a principle that you all learned many years ago: 'He who spares the rod of discipline actually hates his son, but he who loves him is diligent to discipline him.'

John did not interpret the "rod" verse as requiring spankings or physical discipline. But he made clear that firm discipline of some sort is essential. He noted there were many studies on the subject and that they "clearly demonstrate that the kind of parent that produces the child with the greatest sense of self-worth and self-respect with the greatest ability to conform to the authority of those who have authority over them and to get along with other people is the parent who is a firm disciplinarian and who backs this up with a consistent demonstration of love, concern, and support. We must love our children, and be their closest friend, but this love must be accompanied by firm, fair, and consistent discipline."[12]

Another way the Yates ministered to families was inviting others to join in their family life. "We became a part of their family," the Trakowskis said. Jean and Al saw the Yates family up close. "They taught their kids independence," Jean said. "One time we were at their home for a meeting, and a couple of their kids were crying upstairs. I offered to go to them. Susan said, 'they're kissed, they're tucked in, they're prayed over, they'll be okay.'"

The Trakowskis also watched the Yates's kids from time to time. For a stretch of four or five years, they hosted the Yates's oldest two boys at their beach house for a week. "Each of them would bring in their bags and unpack everything. Then they would come to us and say, 'what can we do to help?'" The boys would set the table, do some chores, and ask what else they could do.

Jean remembers one time when the Yates's oldest son, who was about twelve at the time, told them that he could take them out to dinner. *"Pick any place*, he told us." Jean smiled. "Well, we didn't often go out for pizza, so that's what we picked. When we got to the pizza parlor, John went right up to the hostess and said four were in his party. After we ate, he tallied the tip and paid."

The Yates did more than teach about marriage and parenting, they lived an open family life, sharing it with their community and leading by example—an example that, to this day, continues to attract young families.

Love Between The Pastor and His People

"After John and Susan came, it was a love affair." Those were the words of nearly-ninety-year-old Frances Long. "The church has always loved them." Many others shared similar sentiments.

Another long-time church member, Virginia Watson, pointed out that a corollary is also true: "John loves us."

Virginia considered for a moment. Her eyes lit up with a memory. "One morning, not long before my husband Frank died, John called and asked if we'd be home that day. It came out of the blue. I told him we'd be glad to see him."

"Great," John said. "I'll stop by for a few minutes."

"You could stay for a meal. Do you want me to make lunch?"

"No, please don't do anything special."

John came and sat with the Watsons for half an hour. He visited, prayed with them, and left. He didn't ask for anything. He didn't have an agenda.

But Virginia knew why he'd come. It was obvious that he cared for them. He was thinking Frank might not be around much longer.

Of course, as the church grew, John could not always apply such a personal touch. He recognized the limits of his capacity. This meant that he needed to enlist the help of others, and many volunteered over the years.

The church's staff also had an important role to play. After a few years at the church, Judy Thomsen decided to stop her catering work and consider working at The Falls Church. She asked John if he might bring her on as a secretary.

"John was quiet," Judy said. "Then he grinned and said, 'You think we'll still be friends?'"

Judy nodded and signed up for the job.

She worked alongside him for three years. She helped organize his calendar and type his doctoral thesis. After he had cornea transplants in both eyes, she helped produce projections of his sermons as he worked. "I saw him up close and personal," Judy said. "He's everything you think he'd be. He's so genuine."

John made himself available to everyone in the church. Judy remembers his Tuesday open door policy. Anyone could come by to talk with John during certain windows of time. "It was a special thing," Judy said. "Lots of people would come."

John also showed his love for newcomers. In the early 2000s, a recent widow came to the church. She and a few others started ministering to the widows in the church. She'd been going to The Falls Church for a while when, one Sunday after church, John introduced himself. "Tell me what you do for the widows," he said. "I know that there are four of you."

"Well," she said, "why don't you and Susan come over for dinner. I'll invite the widows."

"We would love that."

When the night of the dinner came, the woman told John as he came in, "This is the first time I've entertained and hosted since I lost my husband Larry."

About ten minutes later, John walked into the kitchen. "He said to me, *tell me what Larry used to do, and I'll do it.*"

Tears come to the widow's eyes, just remembering it. "Then I knew I had found a new home," she said. "I've been here ever since."

7

Five Things About
A Thriving Church

Did it ever occur to you that Christ didn't set up a program for the church? He
didn't establish a bureaucracy or a series of committees as a strategy for changing the
world. He simply changed people who have changed the course of history. A concern
of Jesus' was that the people's lives be changed, that they have, first of all, a change
of heart; second, a change of attitude; and finally, changes in their behavior. Those
changes were to shape the future destiny of mankind.
John Yates, March 7, 1982, *Follow the King*

Cities attract people and grow. Schools grow. Churches grow. It's
not the growth itself that matters most. What matters is what, exactly,
the growing organization becomes, and in the context of a church, that
means that people should be changing. The church should be leading
people to be more like Christ, building them up, so that they might
bring the good news to others. Preaching can bring about this kind of
change, but real change takes more than an hour on Sunday mornings.
It takes community, fellowship, and teaching. It has to be personal.
And that's exactly what it was in the 1980s and 1990s at The Falls
Church.[13] To understand the conflict to come, and how the people at
The Falls Church reacted, it helps to understand how they had changed
and had grown together as a family.

1. A Calling to be Different and Make a Difference

Every newcomer took an introductory course called the discovery class. Al and Jean Trakowski, the couple who came to The Falls Church after twenty years at another Episcopal church, attended the very first discovery class taught by John Yates.

"It was an introduction to Christian doctrine," Jean Trakowski said. "It was ten, maybe twelve, people. We would sit in a ring. Every meeting was a potluck. It was like family." The teaching wasn't light, either. "John made it clear," Jean said, "no one should come because this was a historic church; they came for the teachings of Christ." After that first class, the Trakowskis hosted the next twelve discovery classes.

"The Holy Spirit moved through John in a mighty way," Virginia Watson said. "He taught everything—classes on praying and on studying the Bible, and even the newcomers' class. He would have pictures of everyone and put them on his wall so he could memorize their names."

Not only did John give this personal invitation and teaching about what the church believed, but he also provided a clear view of how members were called to be different: "When a group of people in a local community come to love the Lord and love one another, and they're serious about counter-cultural, radical discipleship, and they realize God is calling them to be different and follow Christ in radical ways, that is an incredibly powerful presence in the local community."

This set-apart identity forged tighter bonds among the newcomers. John used a classic image to show the church what they were meant to be once they left the sanctuary:

> We Americans live in a nation that has been consistently salted by Christians throughout our national history, and that is why our nation has been able to aim steadfastly towards justice and freedom for all.
>
> But in every generation the need for true Christian saltiness

continues. Being a salty Christian, being a salty church, is not something we do when we gather here on Sundays. *Here* we are like salt in a salt*shaker*. No, the true work of the church is in between Sundays, out in the world, hidden, in the office, the neighborhood . . . the school . . . the home. Wherever Christian people are, there is the salt of the earth.

The church is to be salt, not sugar. It will not do for any of us to be overly conciliatory with society. We are to be different. We're to be in, but not of. We're of a higher, greater kingdom; we're to be Christ-like. There are many immoralities and injustices right now in our day which we must speak out against. A Christian who doesn't speak out and stand up against injustice, immorality, evil, dishonesty—is like a physician who refuses to visit his patients. But, in our outspokenness, we are also to be full of grace and love, not condemning but attracting all to come join in the feast which the Lord has prepared for us all. A salty Christian is a winsome person.[14]

The church would later capture this image with its mission statement: *To make Christ King in our lives and in the lives of others*. It used the visual shown on the following page to make the point clear.

2. Effective Preaching and Teaching

The Falls Church has always been at its best when the Holy Spirit works through the preacher in the pulpit. But these sermons also began to spread beyond the church's walls. Frank Watson led the "lick and stick group." He and others transcribed, edited, and printed the sermons. Each week the prior week's sermon was available on racks in the church. "These copies would vanish from the racks," one member said. The lick and stick group also mailed the sermons around, including to kids who had grown up in the church and gone to college.

SOME QUALITIES WHICH ARE OFTEN CHARACTERISTIC:

I. When Christ is Not Allowed to be King of a Church

factions
dry worship
dusty Bibles

bickering
gossip
judgmentalness

lack of vision
involvement is mostly out of duty
small impact upon members daily life
joylessness
meager lay ministry
closeminded-leadership
little sense of mission

II. When Christ is King of a Church

not perfect but progressing
growing
enthusiasm
healings occurring

keen sense of mission
joyful worship
persecution
differences accepted

true sense of love for one another
Bible study/prayer groups multiplying
leadership, above all, seeking God's will
gifts of Holy Spirit in operation
multiple ministries developing
deployment of missionaries
people are coming to faith in Christ

An image that The Falls Church used to show its mission statement.

One such student had been receiving these copies of sermons for a while at her dorm. "They stacked up," she remembered. "I never read them. I'd stopped going to church. But one day I was feeling kind of down. So I picked one up, and it made all the difference. I found a church. I am back again."

Who knows which sermon she picked up, but almost any of them could have helped her hear God's voice—a voice that could be faint for a college student struggling through the weeds of competing ideologies. Maybe the sermon she found was like this one from February 6, 1983:

> We should seek to always understand completely the meaning of what the Bible teaches. But sometimes like Simon Peter we won't understand and we just have to push out into deep water trusting God even though we don't understand. Now let's be clear about this. God wants us to understand the meaning of His word. God is not anti-intellectual.

St. Paul writes to Timothy, 'Think over what I say, for the Lord will grant you understanding in every thing.' (2 Tim. 2:7) God doesn't call us to mindless faith. And if a Christian simply says, 'Well, if that's what the Bible says' or 'If that's what the minister says then I'll do it,' he's not using his mind and is treading a dangerous pathway.

But dear friends I don't think *that* is our problem. Our problem today is that all too often we miss out on the blessings and we don't see the power of God at work in our lives because *we worship reason*. And we place too much emphasis on our intellect. Sometimes like Simon Peter we just have to push out into deep water trusting that God will be faithful even though we don't understand.

The writer of Proverbs says, 'Trust in the Lord with all your heart. Lean not unto your own understanding.' (Proverbs 3:5-6) Don't rely upon your ability to understand. One translation says, 'Never rely on what you think you know, trust in the Lord.' And trust in God's word.

Too often we 'sophisticated' Christians approach the words of God in Holy Scripture as though we were the authority and the Bible were subject to our interpretation. Whereas actually the word of God is our authority and we come under the authority of it.[15]

That concluding statement—the Bible as our authority—became the dividing line within the Episcopal Church in years to come. Yates's teaching never wavered from it, and The Falls Church continued to mature in its faith in this authority.

In addition to edifying with his sermons, Yates recommended books to the church. He suggested great works by C.S. Lewis, *Celebration of Discipline* by Richard Foster, and many others. Beyond Sunday mornings, these books deepened the members' walks with Christ.

Yates extolled Christian books so much that, when one church member, Francis Viscount, mentioned that he'd like to run a bookstore when he retired, Yates seized the opportunity: "Why don't you start one here in the church? You could share space with the library." Francis loved the idea and soon acted on it. He obtained a sales license, book distributor accounts, and everything else he needed to open for business. The signal was clear: the church was a place to study and learn.

3. A Tight-Knit Community

Church fellowship halls can be awkward places. People stand around, sipping coffee, making small talk. It was different in Nicholson Hall.

"We knew every face," the Shaffermans remembered. "There was coffee hour every Sunday."

There was also Christmas in the Fellowship Hall. Nothing brings families together like holidays. People would bring turkeys and presents. They exchanged gifts and sang carols. "It was pot-luck living," recalls the Yates's daughter, Allison. "The church was like an extension of our home."

Much of the congregation's growing community could be seen in a once-a-year event that forced them into close proximity: Shrinemont. No one who attended the church in the 1980s talks long without mentioning the church retreat at Shrinemont.

Steve and Nancy Skancke went to Shrinemont for the first time in 1982. About 75 people went that year. The next year, the Skanckes found themselves in charge of the retreat. "We formed a huge committee and made it festive," Steve said. "We invited everyone to our home and ate mussels from Nantucket."

Then 250 came to the next year's retreat. The following year, in 1984, the attendees surged to 650.

"Many of these were newcomers," Steve said. "At Shrinemont they'd be in small groups. Everyone had an obligation to volunteer in some way, too. And so, when people came back, they knew each other."

Getting away from the church property also helped lower everyone's guard. An unusual element permeated these weekends and the church: pure and simple fun. Ask anyone who participated in church retreats such as Shrinemont, and they will immediately smile and start recounting an exceptionally funny experience or story or skit. They laugh in pure enjoyment of one another—a hallmark that remains true of the church. The Yates's daughter Allison remembers well the retreat skits, usually embarrassing the rector in one way or another. John and Susan took it in good stride. They did not take themselves too seriously, and the openness at Shrinemont helped the church grow closer. "People saw my parents wearing blue jeans," Allison said. They were far from the formal robes of the historic Falls Church.

By the late 1980s, so many people were coming to Shrinemont that they had to stop hosting the main events in the ballroom. They moved to an outside pavilion that could fit everyone. People rented houses in the area so they could attend. "We had the streak," the Shaffermans said. "Sixteen years straight."

The Shrinemont retreats were not the only source of the church's joyous spirit. One Christmas, the Henneberg family heard their doorbell ring. They came to the door but no one was in sight. On their porch sat a cage. In the cage, unharmed, was a squirrel and a note.

The note: "Merry Christmas — the Yates."

After a week, the Hennebergs returned the favor. They left the empty cage on the Yates's doorstep, rang the doorbell, and fled the scene. The cage had a note. "Thank you for the gift. We were quite hungry."

The church family knew how to have fun. It also knew how to share in life's challenges. Another important component of fellowship was small groups and focused ministry. Almost everyone who attended The Falls Church in the 1980s explained that, even as the church numbers swelled, they had strong bonds with those in their small groups. Some called them "home churches"—showing how they believed church to be far more than a place they went on Sunday mornings. The Holy Spirit moved from Washington's colonial brick building and into people's homes. These groups brought great growth and community.

This community was built of both men and women. A common irony of churches is that men fill the positions of highest leadership while, through the ranks, women are far more involved. It's women who are more likely to be in small groups. It has long been women who lay the church's groundwork.

Why? Maybe because church wasn't cool for men.

John Yates changed that. Over decades when more and more men settled into permanent adolescence, Yates went against the grain. He didn't try to be counter-cultural. He just explained what the Bible taught as the culture drifted away from it. And what the Bible taught was maturity.

God made the world to need mature men to work in it, and to work together. They need to meet regularly, to share in their struggles, to keep each other accountable.

The men's ministry met at least once every month. Yates brought in high quality speakers, and a huge group of men showed up. He was focused on getting men back in the church.

This focus not only benefited the church over time, but it also came to protect Yates. Rather than operate in isolation, he maintained multiple accountability groups—friends and professional peers. One year in the mid-1990s, Yates taught about how men should pray. This later led to his book, *How a Man Prays for His Family*. At the time, Yates's teaching inspired Ramsey Gilchrist, then-chaplain on the Senior PGA Tour, to encourage him to ask men to pray for him. They would set aside one day a month to fast and pray for things Yates requested. About sixty men volunteered. The number doubled over time.

To this day, a group of nearly two hundred men coordinate so that someone is fasting and praying for Yates every single day of the month. As Yates says, these men "have walked through the years with me, carrying my burdens with me, sharing with me the major events in my life." And the men have done so gratefully, considering it a privilege and gaining insights into how to be more faithful and thoughtful men of God themselves. The group paints a picture of the church as the Body of Christ. Everyone was in this family together.

4. Discipleship of Youth

"If the church isn't capturing young people of today," John Yates says, "then the church of tomorrow will die." He believed firmly, drawing on his own experience as a youth leader, that the church needed to be reaching out to young people and laying out a vision of Christ that would capture their imaginations and bring them into the family of God. He knew the stakes in the region. "Life in Washington, DC, is difficult. It is full of pressures. No one ever has enough time. As we try to help families and individuals, and as we work with other young pastors, we encourage them about the priority of time alone with God, and time with family."

This teaching attracted parents in droves. Yates needed leaders to help minister to the children. He found some amazing young men. Several have led the youth ministry over the years and each has been outstanding in their understanding of how to communicate with teens. Among them are: John Burley, John Butin, Jeff Taylor, David Healing, and most recently, the inimitable Jim Byrne.

Over the years these leaders did four things.

First, they established a discipleship mentality. Middle school kids don't listen much. High school kids don't want to listen to parents. Who do they care about? *College* kids. And who do college kids listen to? Young adults.

That became the model. Young adults mentored college students.

College students mentored high schoolers, who mentored those younger. This approach was good not only for the younger kids, but it also helped keep the older kids engaged. They had an important role. It made them invested. They learned discipleship by doing.

Second, the leaders made things fun. Something different happened every time the youth met. One time a youth leader brought in a couple of sheep. "One of them pooped on stage—a sheep, not a kid," recalled one church member. "The kids had a lot of fun with that."

Third, the music was great. Guitars, drums, and more. The kids were part of the band.

Fourth, the leadership decided to take the youth on a road trip. In 1989, they rented five vans and a truck and plotted a course to South Dakota. This was before cell phones. They had CB radios to communicate among them.

The trip needed other parents to come along. One girl convinced her dad, Don Dusenbury, to join them. She told him, "All the kids think you're cool." That did it. Because of work, he had to fly out to meet them in Wisconsin. He arrived and marveled that they'd made it that far. He helped improve the organization—more maps, more radios. He filled a need. They called him "Doc Don."

Filling that need, going with those kids, serving and praying with them, brought Doc Don to a personal faith in Jesus Christ. He'd gone to an Episcopal boarding school, with chapel every day. "I'd been to enough church for my life," he said. So when his family first started going to The Falls Church, he didn't join them often. His wife Angela would take the kids to church, leaving him behind to read the paper and catch up on work.

That changed after the youth road trip. And a decade later, Don's son became a youth minister at the church. Don was elected to the vestry. "I'm convinced it was because the church thought they were voting for my son," Don joked.

Generational lines had blurred. It was clear that the church's focus on children had strengthened the whole enterprise—from the youngest to the oldest. And over the coming decades, it would not be unusual to have five hundred young people in attendance at the Sunday afternoon and Sunday evening Crossroads and Cornerstone gatherings. The impact was profound.

5. Growth

The Falls Church did not start getting attention because that was its goal. It got attention because of the amazing changes and growth underway. People were responding in powerful ways.

By 1984, as The Falls Church grew like wildfire, signs of tension with the Episcopal Church appeared. An article in *Christianity Today* brought this to national attention:

> Since the 1960s, The Episcopal Church has been sliding steadily in membership. The trend bottomed out last year, when the denomination gained 27,000 new people. But that long-sought turnaround came much quicker, and much stronger, in the Northern Virginia suburbs of Washington, D.C. There, a fertile mixture of evangelical preaching, charismatic renewal, and liturgical worship is producing steady growth. . . .
>
> "When Rector John Yates arrived in 1979, he was asked by the church board to emphasize outreach, evangelism, and renewal. 'When we started moving in that direction, it was very difficult for a number of traditional people in the church,' he says. 'They resented Bibles in the pews and a new emphasis from the pulpit.' Nevertheless, Falls Church's attendance doubled to 700 in three years. [The number of small groups] increased from 2 to 20 under Yates's gentle prodding. Even more significant, to him, is the number of men assuming spiritual leadership through several men's Bible studies. . . .

An article about The Falls Church in Christianity Today in 1984.
The photo shows John Yates at the historic church property.

"The Episcopal Church hierarchy welcomes the growth despite some wariness over charismatic renewal. . . . Traditionally thought of as the bridge between Protestantism and Catholicism, The Episcopal Church is in the process of adding a new dimension to its identity. As parishioners take their faith more seriously, and a second and third generation of evangelical priests begin to lead, *changes are taking place that could alter the course of the entire denomination.*"[16]

And so they would. But first, there was more expanding and more thriving to do.

8

Five More Things
About A Thriving Church

There are many reasons why people come to our church, but it's the people, the dear people, that are the reason why people stay.

John Yates

The 1990s were pretty good years in America. The decade followed the economic downturns and the neon of the 1980s. It was before 9/11, the war on terror, and the financial collapse. Stocks were rising and the country was growing. We hurtled toward a new millennium with excited energy.

The Falls Church reflected a similar kind of energy, full of life and growth and changed lives.

6. Vision for Physical Space

The growth at The Falls Church brought mostly good things, but it was not without its challenges. One was simply a matter of space.

"We were bursting at the seams," Steve Skancke said. Every Sunday, folding chairs filled the aisles in the old historic church. But that wasn't enough.

"We could not fit in the pews with our coats on," said Virginia Watson. "We either had to leave our coats in the car, or fold them up and put them under the seat."

The fire chief had limits for how many people could fill the building. The church had to start turning away people at the doors.

In 1985, a man named Charlie Bennett approached the church stiffly one Sunday morning, with canes in his hands and braces on his legs. He had polio. He also had a seat in the U.S. House of Representatives. Bennett had been a leading Democrat in Congress for decades. He had sponsored legislation in the 1950s that put "In God We Trust" on U.S. coins.

But that Sunday morning, there was no seat to be found for Charlie Bennett. The sanctuary was overflowing, and so Bennett, like many others, could only watch the service on closed-circuit television in the fellowship hall.

Clearly, the church needed more worship space. But the need was deeper, too. Yates explained why in a sermon:

> There are new programs, new classes. There are some old programs and old classes that are newly invigorated. There are some new emphases. There's a completely new staff; the budget has doubled; the leadership in many areas has shifted. Things have changed and certain problems are inherent in such changes.
>
> Whenever you have growth, the result is that there are many unfamiliar faces and the space becomes cramped. All of our rooms are used for a multitude of purposes. As new people take on leadership, many old-timers are grateful, but some are a little resentful or hurt. One of the biggest challenges we face is to maintain active involvement on the part of all those in the church and at the same time assimilate those who come in new to the family. Another problem, or challenge, is to know where we're going over the long run. If we continue to grow, what does that say about our space?

As the need for more space grew, Sam Thomsen sat down with John for several days. "I went to his little inner sanctum," Sam said. "It was downstairs in his house. I brought my mini-computer—small for that time, anyway—and took notes. John laid out a five-year vision for a building plan. Everything he envisioned came to pass."

But building takes more than a plan. It requires money, and raising money is never easy. A new sanctuary would require a fundraising effort.

At the same time, some members of the church were reluctant to see changes to the historic property. It was wrapped up in the other changes that Yates had brought. Jean Trakowski remembered the words of one older member. "He told me, '*I knew it*,' and he waved his finger like this." Jean waved her weathered finger triumphantly. "*I knew that man would want to do something like this.*"

There was also nostalgia about how tight-knit the church was in its smaller, historic building. Jean remembered another member who had come from a megachurch in California worrying about the new, larger building. "It will never be the same," the man told her.

Yates had seen this danger on the horizon. A few years earlier, he'd addressed it from the pulpit. These words would echo loudly decades later.

A church *building* is a means by which a group of people can come together and in a wonderful way worship God. But, dear friends, it is possible for people to end up worshipping the building rather than God, and to be more concerned with the place of worship than with the worship of God himself. I believe that I probably love this building as much as anyone in the Parish. I would hate to ever see anything keep us from worshipping in this place. But, let us be careful that the building doesn't become an idol.

Whenever we are more concerned with a particular liturgy or group of hymns than we are with prayer and praise of God himself, whenever we are more concerned with Episcopalianism than with the wider Body of Christ worldwide itself, or whenever we are more concerned with a church building than we are concerned with the good of the church, then we are guilty of idolatry as sure as if we were bowing down before graven images.

It is easy for a minister to worship the worship or to worship the sermon. The choir spends a lot of time preparing music, but music can become an idol. And the challenge for us is when we come together to be so prepared that we can turn our hearts to God and simply worship God.[17]

In the end, attached as people were to the historic church, there was simply no question that The Falls Church needed more space. A few people left the church over it, but the vast majority supported the plan to build a new sanctuary.

The church moved forward, navigating the challenges of fundraising. The money needed for construction took away funds from other outreach ministries. Some in the church had hoped to reach a point where they could give half of the church's money for ministry elsewhere. "We got up to 44%," one member said. "But that had to go down to build a new building. If it's God's plan," he added, "money will not be an issue."

Nor would the city planning committee or architectural decisions be insurmountable. The church managed to get the city's approval with a few design changes. They also adopted a more modern layout. They had originally agreed on a traditional, rectangular basilica in the northeast of the property. Yates went on sabbatical in the summer of 1987. When he came back, the whole plan had changed. The sanctuary was now going to be a circular building on the southern part of the property. "I knew I wasn't running things!" Yates said.

The circular building became known fondly as the Episcodome. It could seat nearly one thousand people, and its brick walls and bright windows and comfortable pews offered a brilliant space for worship. The church also spent a large sum on a custom-fitted organ for the new sanctuary.

The place hosted not only worship on Sundays, but also major events in the life of the church. The first such major event was a wedding—the wedding of the Yates's oldest daughter Allison.

Fitting with their church-as-family life, the Yates put the invitation in the church bulletin for everyone to come. The sanctuary filled to the brim on the big day in May 1994. This was the occasion for the new sanctuary and its organ to have a shining moment.

It did not go entirely according to plan. "The organ, which was still new, had a mind of its own that day," John said. "We all marched in to wonderful singing of a hymn of praise, but when the hymn was over, the organ wasn't finished! Instead of an 'amen' from the organ bench, it let out a long, wailing, blaring cry."[18]

Allison described the sound from the "big, fancy organ" as resembling a "sad cow with air draining out." This was a pivotal moment. The crowd fell silent and tension rose as the organ's sound faded.

What would happen? Would the bride cry?

No. A first laugh escaped someone's lips, and soon the whole crowd had burst out in laughter.

The rest of the wedding went beautifully.

The sanctuary at The Falls Church, built in the early 1990s.

7. Ministry By The People

The Falls Church had a very small staff in the 1980s. But its ministries and programs were growing by leaps and bounds, propelled by volunteers. Lay people had great responsibility. A women's group covered at least twenty different tasks for the church. As the church continued to grow, there was room for even more.

Throughout his first decade at the church, John Yates encouraged the congregation to get more involved in ministering to each other. "We've got to recover an exciting idea—that every Christian is a minister. Martin Luther opened the Bible to the layman. Now the Holy Spirit is opening up ministry to the layman."[19]

Such calls for ministry became common in Yates's sermons. One Sunday he focused on the importance of such work by the average church member. At the end of the sermon, he called on the congregation to stand—"stand if you affirm the calling of Jesus Christ to ministry."

When pastors call people to stand in a church, that's what they do. But this time there was an exception. A dedicated Falls Church member and well-known author, Os Guinness, was irritated. He refused to stand.

Yates noticed this, of course. He found Os after the service.

"Why didn't you stand?" John asked.

"You don't recognize the importance of ministry *outside* the church." Os's words stirred something that had been bothering John for a while.

"I wasn't teaching the ministry of working men and women," John remembers. "The lesson is that the pastor does not have all the answers." He clenched his fists for emphasis, as if holding tight this critical insight. John never forgot the importance of his congregants' ministry outside the church after that. No matter where Christ's people were, in any day job and in any conversation, they served as a royal priesthood (1 Peter 2:9).

Ministries inside the church continued to grow and involve many members. For some, it would begin with a gentle word from John or Susan Yates. "John and Susan had millions of ideas," Jean Trakowski said. "They would put them into people." They did not micro-manage, but trusted in the gifts of the Spirit working through everyone in the church. In other words, John and Susan would plant an idea in a church member and see it grow. This was deliberate. The Yates understood—from Ephesians 4:12—that change percolated up from the members, rather than top-down from the staff and its programs. "Our people," John said, "they're so smart. Part of my job is just to identify the needs and let our people come up with ways to address them."

Many fruits of the church grew organically from inspired members. The Falls Church member Gary Haugen founded International Justice Mission, which grew into a global organization with hundreds of lawyers, investigators, social workers, and community activists who fight human trafficking and protect the poor from violence in the developing world.

Another member, Ludy Green, founded Second Chance Employment Services, which led over 500 women out of abusive households. Ms. Green recounted the role that a meeting with John Yates had in her efforts. "I am convinced that if Rev. Yates had not prayed so fervently for me," Ms. Green wrote, "I would never have had the courage to do any of these things." Many other Falls Church members have similarly carried out great work for the kingdom of God, supported by their home church.

But amidst such successes, the church could not forget to care for its own. Every church with people in it has brokenness and suffering in it.

In the early 1990s, soon after building the new sanctuary, Yates became concerned that the church wasn't pastoring its people well. He shared this with the vestry. "I fear we are bleeding in a few places," he told them. "People have needs that aren't being met."

Yates didn't propose his own answers. He knew this issue could not be solved alone. He called for help, as he often did when he recognized a gap. The vestry formed a committee to study the problem.

They came back a month later. "John, we're not bleeding," they said. "We're hemorrhaging." Many members' needs—ranging from serious personal struggles to difficulties with normal daily tasks—were going unmet.

This was worse than John expected. It took him aback. "So . . . what do we do?"

The vestry tasked two members with developing ideas.

One of the members was Elizabeth Brunner. She and her husband Mike have the look of a couple that has grown together. Both are fine-featured and graceful, with intensity and intelligence in their eyes.

"I don't know how the vestry committee got my name," Elizabeth said. "They called me about the issue. I said, 'sounds interesting.' I ended up taking a leave of absence from my job. I'd been working as a psychologist in the Arlington school system for 23 years." Elizabeth's leave of absence was part of an extensive plan she developed in cooperation with the vestry for a "pastoral care team."

At first John was nervous about this idea. The concern was not about Elizabeth's ability—she had proven that in her career, and she even had the familiar trait of being a classmate of John's in college. The concern was the unique challenges of pastoring. Still, John let Elizabeth have a try with setting it up her way. The pastoral care team made a phone number available for anyone in the church to call when they needed help. The team would coordinate volunteer church members for help, or make recommendations where the parishioner could find what they needed.

"It didn't take long for us to realize this was more than a part-time job," Elizabeth said. "I took it on full-time."

When asked if she was paid, Elizabeth smiled, unsurprised by the question. "No."

"They offered to pay her," her husband Mike added, "but she turned it down."

"We got an office in the church," Elizabeth continued. "It was important that we had a physical presence. At first it was just me, three days a week, with several volunteers who came in for half days."

In the beginning, only a dozen or so called the number per month. But the word spread. "People heard that we were doing good work, and more and more came with their requests. It was a gradual but steady increase."

This pastoral care process was simple in theory, but hard to manage. The team circulated a sheet to the full congregation, asking people to list their skills that could help others. It ranged from driving people places to financial advice to prayers for those who lost loved ones. The sheet was called the "Storehouse of Service." It was not computerized at the time, so Elizabeth and her team had to create an elaborate system for connecting people. "We also maintained strict confidentiality for anyone who contacted us with needs."

"The routine things were handled by other volunteers on the team," Mike added. "They drove people, delivered flowers, and things like that. Elizabeth handled the hard stuff. Whenever there was a call about a daughter cutting herself, or an affair, or a brain tumor, or depression—Elizabeth handled it." Mike paused at the gravity of these concerns. "The issues did not weigh her down, but the volume did."

"I wasn't offering therapy or counseling," Elizabeth clarified. "It was more like an initial intake meeting. I would assess the problem, and if needed, refer it to someone. I had a strong network of clinical practitioners in the area, so I could point members to the right person."

Most of the people who came were individuals with issues. There were a lot of cases of clinical depression. A few with bipolar symptoms. "A lot of married couples came, too," Elizabeth said. "I had an advantage. I was independent, and I wasn't a 'counselor.' I was more like a coach. I would meet with couples a time or two, so I could get the big picture of the issues. Sometimes I would send them on to a counselor. But sometimes I was able to identify something to help immediately. They weren't afraid to talk to me. I mean, I was kind of answerable to John, but I was not paid. I was not staff. I was just doing pastoral care."

Elizabeth declined to give examples of how her work helped people. "I don't want to give any specifics, because the people I helped would probably know what it was about."

Even now, Mike has no idea who she talked to over the years. "They'll come up to me in church and mention something as if I know about it. I don't. Elizabeth kept it confidential." Mike smiled. "She knows where the bodies are buried."

Elizabeth served in this leading role—full-time and unpaid—for over twenty years. She stepped down in 2012. "It's hard," she said. "People still want to talk to me, but I'm not in that position anymore. But I still know the stories, and I still care about them."

Few churches can offer a similar service. Most don't have the money. Most don't have someone like Elizabeth, willing to do such challenging work for zero pay. Still, Elizabeth always spoke to other churches when they wanted to learn how she ran the program. "I remember people coming to me and saying, *I've never seen a church that cares for people the way you do.*"

The program now has two paid staff and over 20 volunteers. The pastoral care team meets needs of all kinds in the church. Every week, Yates receives a report about their work. "It lists 40 or 50 pastoral contacts," he explained. "It says what the need was, and how the pastoral care team responded to it. This is an amazing ministry, and it happened without the clergy leading it."

It could be easy to write this program off as a unique thing that few churches could provide, given the resources required. But the commitment of people like Elizabeth shows something bigger. It shows that the church and its teaching could inspire a talented psychologist to dedicate herself to serving people, to serving the

Kingdom, just as Christ might have done.

Another ministry at the church also showed this kind of dedication. From the time he was young, Yates had experienced and had a deep faith in the healing power of the Holy Spirit. He taught about this from time to time, and attempted to establish a healing ministry. John Parke gave good leadership to this ministry in the early days, but it didn't thrive as Yates believed it should.

Finally, driven by frustration or perhaps divine revelation, on a Sunday morning in the mid-nineties, Yates preached on the topic. He told the congregation that he believed that God wanted to establish a stronger healing ministry in the church, but that his efforts in that direction had largely been ineffective. He said, "If you want to see this established, you're going to have to do it yourself. I don't know how to do it but I think you people probably do, so I'm leaving it in your hands."

Yates received more response to that sermon than just about any other sermon he ever preached, and a gifted team under the leadership of Chuck and Nancy Cook was formed to begin praying about how to move forward in healing ministry. This became one of the most dynamic ministries in the church, now overseen by a member of the clergy, Kathleen Christopher. Healing services regularly report various forms of healing, and healing teams have gone out from the church both near and abroad. The church has hosted healing conferences to prepare leaders from scores of other churches to bind up the sick, the hurt, and the brokenhearted. It is ministry by the people.

8. Outreach and Missions

In his first years at the church, Yates criticized American Episcopalians for letting other people do the missionary work in other cultures. "If we do not commit ourselves to missionary work, we will die having been disobedient to Christ in what might be the most important command he ever gave us." Yates made this calling concrete: "I would like to see—and this is a challenge—40 percent of our parish budget clearly marked for ministry outside our parish within the next few years. We *must* become a missions-minded parish if we're going to experience the blessing of God in our midst."[20]

Two years later Yates reported a good start in this area. He explained that giving was "a much bigger question than what 600 people are going to pledge to The Falls Church. We are just a small group of people, but we can do a significant work. In the last ten years over $200,000 has gone from this parish into missionary work. That's just a beginning. I want to pledge something to you as your rector. I personally am not going to be satisfied until we are giving away half of our budget for the purposes of Christian missions, and we are responsibly seeing how it is used so that food and clothing go to the needy, wells are dug and water is provided for those who are thirsty, and the Gospel is brought to those who have not heard it. I'm not going to be satisfied until every one of us has learned principles of conscientious stewardship and has received training in personal evangelism."[21]

Of course, effective missions required more than money. In 1987, Yates made his first trip to Africa to visit with church leaders and missionaries in Kenya and Uganda. He brought his fifteen-year-old daughter Allison with him. It was a profound experience for both of them. Allison remembers visiting a school where many of the children had never seen a blue-eyed, blonde-haired girl before. They sang and danced in welcome as she and her father arrived. John laid a foundation stone for a new church—partnering with an African pastor who looked nothing like him on the outside but very much like him on the inside.

"These are our people," Allison remembers thinking at the time. Little did she or John know how true that would be in the years ahead. These partnerships with Christian brothers and sisters in Africa would bear much fruit.

John was far from alone among church members in his direct

engagement with missions work. Charlie Powell, the close friend of John's, had moved to France for missions. He returned in the late eighties, and his heart was on fire for spreading the gospel internationally. He became the church's first Missions Director in 1990. Over four years in that position, he established English-as-a-second-language (ESOL) courses. He started an inner-city ministry project. And he launched a mission in Kazakhstan.

Charlie had been in Kazakhstan in 1990, when the Soviet Union collapsed. "At that time, the Kazakh people were in the grips of Soviet Russia," Charlie said. "There were millions of these peaceful, fun-loving Muslims in Central Asia who had never even heard the gospel." He explained that there were Christian Russian churches in the country, but the Russians did not mix with the Kazakh people. There was also no Kazakh translation of the Bible. "We had an opportunity to reach these people."

Charlie and the church set sights on the city of Aktau, the country's main port on the Caspian Sea. It was a burgeoning city. The Russians, having discovered uranium deposits nearby, built communist-bloc buildings to house workers who mined the resource and ran the nuclear power station. This meant economic growth and openness to international travel, but not necessarily to the gospel. Charlie hoped to change that. In 1993, he led a mission to Aktau with ten others from The Falls Church.

The trip was a success—full of new contacts and interesting conversations. On the last day, they met with the Russian mayor of Aktau. Charlie remembers the meeting well. "The mayor told one of the young men from our church that if he wanted to come back, and if he would teach English in a local college, the city would pay for his apartment and cover his expenses. It wasn't a religious thing. They wanted to build bridges to the Americans."

The young man was Robert Watkin, and Charlie loved this idea. He thought Robert had the gifts for the missionary job. "He wasn't a pastor," Charlie said. "He was just a young guy who took to the people there. He played the guitar. Everyone liked him.''

Robert was twenty-five years old when he had first visited The Falls Church. He came because a friend invited him. The church was so packed when he arrived that the only seat was in the second row, sitting right below the pulpit rising ten feet above. Despite the crowd, despite the up-front seat, it wasn't uncomfortable. "It was like coming home," Robert said. "John Yates was preaching the gospel in a winsome way." Like others who had joined the church in the years before him, Robert took a discovery class and became deeply involved. "Everything changed," Robert said. He recommitted his life to Christ. He joined the "Salt & Light" ministry group, joined the trip to Kazakhstan, and now faced an offer to move to the country full time.

"I came to Johnny with the idea," Charlie recalled. "I was really excited. Well, Johnny wasn't so sure. He asked me, 'you sure this is a good idea?'" Charlie paused. "He was concerned about sending someone without formal training. But I'd been there. I believed in this."

John eventually agreed to the plan, but the decision to go still was not easy for Robert. Going to Kazakhstan would mean leaving behind friends, family, and his teaching career in the United States. Around that time, Leighton Ford spoke one Sunday at the church. He preached against Christians settling for "too small a thing." Robert found this convicting. He had a unique opportunity to serve God's glory and His global purposes. "I could be like a Christian Navy Seal."

Robert moved to Aktau in March 1994. In his first week, someone invited him to an art exhibition. A woman named Gulnara approached Robert there and told him that she was a believer. This was a great surprise to Robert, as it was understood that there were only a few Christians in the whole country. She asked Robert if he would help teach the Bible to her small group. It was a powerful start.

During Robert's first year in Aktau, John Yates and others visited. On a bright Sunday, the group went with Gulnara to the shore of the Caspian Sea. The water glistened as John, Robert, and Gulnara waded into the gentle waves. John baptized Gulnara there. "I remember so well," he later said, "the amazing experience of baptizing a new believer—as far as we knew, the first in that part of the world—in the Caspian Sea."

Robert stayed in Aktau for five years. A group of missionaries joined him there. But after Robert left, some connections with local leaders were lost. The Kazakh people were beginning to fill positions of leadership in Aktau, and as Muslims, they were less tolerant of Christian missionaries. Just two or three months after Robert left, the missionary group was deported from the country. But, as Charlie Powell said, "the work had been done. Robert was able to plant the seeds that reached thousands."

When Robert returned to The Falls Church, he was a changed man. He asked John about entering seminary. "Robert," John joked, "don't go to seminary. It will only mess you up!" But he continued on a more serious note: "Know why you're going and don't be sidetracked."

Robert did know: his focus was on missions. And when he graduated from Trinity Seminary in 2001, Yates invited him to join the staff at The Falls Church, where he has continued to lead the church in its ongoing and rich missions work.

9. Equipping the Next Generation

In 1993, John Yates had an idea of a program to train youth pastors. He shared his idea with his long-time friend, Doug Holladay. They talked through it, and Doug told John, "You're not thinking big enough. This isn't just about youth ministers."

They prayed together about the idea. They studied and refined the idea. The vision broadened into a yearlong intensive program for recent college graduates. The graduates would not focus on youth ministry, but would learn about God calling men and women to serve Him in the workplace. This meant in Capitol Hill, in business, on K

Street—wherever God called.

John and Doug got others excited about this idea, and the church adopted it as "The Fellows Program."

The program teaches Fellows that every area of life matters to God, not just what they do on Sundays. While the curriculum includes seminary courses in Apologetics and Engaging the Culture, the program involves much more. The Fellows live with host families, work in a professional setting, meet with mentors, and participate in discipleship training, Bible study, and weekly seminars.

For over twenty years, Steve Garber has taught the Fellows and many others about the gift of Christian vocation. His passion—captured in the book *Visions of Vocation*—guides people to serve God in the culture, to know the world and still love the world. It is a mission that many Fellows take with them.

A director manages the many strands and relationships of the Fellows Program. One former director, Morna Comeau, described her role as being like "the balloon man at the zoo—where there's a huge bouquet of balloons, and the balloon man holds it together at the bottom."

Since its founding, the Fellows Program has taught over 250 recent college graduates. As they've completed the program and moved on, they've spread the word to new cities and new churches. Now fellows programs exist at over twenty churches, in many cities and in many denominations, equipping hundreds of college graduates every year to start well in their professional journeys. The impact has been huge. Spending the pivotal post-college year in such programs has transformed Fellows' lives. It has nudged their paths toward serving Christ in their work wherever they go.

But the program brought other benefits—unexpected benefits—to The Falls Church. "It made a huge difference," Molly Shafferman said. "It ups the tempo." These fresh college grads showed up every year, bringing enthusiasm and energy to the church.

Molly served for years as a mentor and matcher—someone who

helped pair Fellows with church members. She explained how the Fellows Program mentors become closely involved in the Fellows' lives, especially the mentors who hosted them for the year in their homes. The Fellows, in turn, serve as mentors for the youth group, discipling high school students about to embark on the same college journey the Fellows had just navigated.

Morna Comeau witnessed how integral this discipleship role was in the life of the church's teenagers. "Just as kids would start to pull away, and start to think their friends are more wise than their parents, in moves a twenty-two-year-old to the house. The kid assumes this person will be their ally, and the parent also trusts this person." The Fellows act as intermediaries between parents and their teens, translating between generations and serving as a powerful example, like an adopted big sibling, in the very home of teenagers. This not only strengthens the church family, but it helps teach the Fellows how important their mentorship could be in the lives of young people.

After six years as the Fellows Program director, Morna Comeau became the director of the Fellows Initiative, which shares best practices with and helps other churches establish and run their own fellows programs.[22] To mark this transition for Morna, ten other families that had hosted Fellows gathered for a celebratory dinner. These families had hosted dozens of Fellows among them. Many of these Fellows, as time passed, married each other and began their own families. And so these ten host families could rejoice together in their twenty-seven "host grandchildren."

Many Fellows also ended up staying at The Falls Church, forming a nucleus of young adults. This presented a new opportunity: Kairos (which means in ancient Greek, a special moment in time that has arrived). Bill Haley founded this young adult ministry in 1996. A former Vestry member, Carol Jackson, described Kairos as "the Yates-authorized, God-given brain child of Bill Haley." Kairos reflected the synergy of John's and Bill's different styles. "Bill was more Baptist than Episcopalian. John saw Bill's Spirit-led heart for the poor in spirit and material goods, and he trusted his vision for a young adult 'kairos' community attuned to the times as we were being called to urban ministry and boots on the ground relationships with those not like us in the Northern Virginia suburbs."

With John's steady support and Bill's leadership, Kairos grew from a small nucleus of like-hearted young adults to a large community of 20 and 30-year-olds with a passion for serving the poor and the wayward in urban centers.

Coming full circle, the Fellows Program also bore fruit reminiscent of John Yates's original idea of training youth ministers. "We didn't expect this," John said, "but over time a few Fellows came to me and wanted to learn more about being an ordained minister. Now a number of them have done that. One of the young men, who was a Fellow, went to seminary. Then we brought him back to The Falls Church to train to be a leader of another church in the area. But he surprised me. He said he wanted to start a *new* church. He asked me, 'what should I do now to prepare?' That was the beginning of the Timothy program."

The Timothy program would become a major church-planting initiative. This could only reach its fullest potential, however, after tensions mounted further with the Episcopal Church.

10. Meaningful Worship

Anyone who has heard a church organ knows the sound. The congregation stands; they flip open the hymn book and sing the verses. Then they sit down.

That's how it had long been at The Falls Church. But just as the Spirit was bringing new people and new life into The Falls Church, so too came new music.

The change didn't happen overnight. Just because someone could play a song on a guitar didn't mean it was ready for the church. "John doesn't do things until they can be done well," said a long-time church member.

Katherine Weller remembered the first time the worship included a more contemporary song. "Before it was always the organ and hymns." Just the organ and hymns. "But one Sunday we sang *Surely, It is God Who Saves Me*. We sang it again the next Sunday. Week after week, we'd sing hymns and then that song." Katherine smiled. "We started to rock a bit. We could sense something. We were changing."

A few people might even lift their hands from time to time. The stiffness of services was breaking loose. At some point a talented dancer wanted to take another step. "Could we start a dance ministry?" she asked John Yates. "John about had a heart attack," Katherine Weller remembered, laughing. But they did it, "and it freed us up." Another step was the Hallelujah Chorus. It was a little band with a piano, guitar, and a couple singers.

Fast-forward thirty years, and The Falls Church worship team involves a full band that has produced several recorded albums. This development reflected that nothing is more important in church life than worship. It's one of the most counter-cultural things that Christians do. It should be true to scripture, joyful, and inspirational. It should help people genuinely enter into God's presence, listen to Him, and give themselves to Him.

Many gifted musicians have led the worship over the years. Marilyn Murchison and Alice and Marvin Crawford came to the church from Presbyterian backgrounds. Wally and Joan Horton came from Missouri Synod Church. Simon and Caryn Dixon came from Holy Trinity Brompton, the Anglican Church that is the home of the worldwide Alpha movement. Simon Dixon is a top-flight concert organist who has given concerts all over the world. He came to the church knowing that it could lose its handmade organ. He said that he was joining the church family to serve, whether he had a fine organ or not.

9

Bubbling Conflict

*Everyone who goes on ahead and does not abide in the teaching of Christ
does not have God. Whoever abides in the teaching has both the Father and
the Son. If anyone comes to you and does not bring this teaching,
do not receive him into your house or give him any greeting,
for whoever greets him takes part in his wicked works.*
2 John 1:9-11

Growth continued unabated at The Falls Church. The addition of
the new sanctuary fueled the church's expansion, as more people came
and could find seats on Sunday morning. Through the 1990s, the
congregation topped 1,000, then 2,000.

Growth does not come without challenges, but usually that
challenge comes from existing limitations—strains imposed by the
growth itself. The Falls Church faced a different kind of challenge. The
vitality brought by the Holy Spirit—the same vitality that had made the
church grow and thrive—was beginning to conflict with the direction
of the Episcopal Church.

Seeds of Conflict

The seeds of conflict had been planted within the Episcopal
Church for many years. It is impossible to pinpoint an exact date when
the conflict began. As an Anglican bishop would later explain, "I
would use a comparison about when a marriage fails and it's hard to

say this is the moment that the marriage—where [the problem] started, but usually the significant, observable phenomena are preceded by smaller things leading up to that."[23]

But a key year was 1989.

Virginia Watson remembers attending the Episcopal General Convention that year. At a committee meeting, debate arose over whether to refer to Jesus as the "unique" son of God. The attending members discussed, and Virginia watched. Someone noted, "we are all sons of God in some way." Another person added that the word "unique" would perhaps make others feel disparaged, as if they were not also unique. In the end, the committee voted against the word "unique."

The decision made Virginia cry. It was the first sign for her of the Episcopal Church believing that Jesus Christ was *a* way, not *the* way.

Another church member, George Hooper, recalls attending the first services ever held at the Washington National Cathedral as part of the National Day of Prayer on May 5, 1994. A clergyman at the Washington National Cathedral was enthusiastic about the idea. The National Day of Prayer, based on a federal statute, invited American people to "turn to God in prayer and meditation at churches, in groups, and as individuals."[24] It was fitting that such a day would be celebrated at the National Cathedral.

George Hooper explained how the event went. "The program opened with a Native American drummer calling us to pray to the Great Spirit. In turn, a Sikh holy man, a Jewish rabbi, a Muslim imam, and perhaps a few others prayed or spoke, with appropriate references to their respective religions. This lineup was interspersed with three hymns from the regular Episcopal hymnal, and a homily by the Cathedral Dean. About halfway into the order of worship, I noticed a distinct pattern which continued throughout the entire program: at no time—not in the opening welcome, or prayers, or hymns, or homily, or benediction—was the name of Jesus Christ proclaimed."

After the program, George had an opportunity to speak with one of the clergy. The man approached George, effervescent with satisfaction, and said he was pleased that the event had been "so ecumenical" and quite well attended.

"It was a fine program," George replied, "but not once in the whole service was the name of Jesus Christ mentioned. Is this not a Christian church?"

The clergyman paused, and not answering directly, swept his arms about and looked up into the Cathedral expanse saying, "But look at this magnificent place. The statuary and symbols of Christianity surround us."

George left the grounds distinctly disappointed—but not surprised at another example of "symbol over substance" in Episcopal leadership.

Beyond the Washington D.C. area, a leader of the Episcopal Church's move away from traditional faith was Bishop John Shelby Spong. He was elected as a bishop in New Jersey in 1979, the same year that John Yates came to The Falls Church. By all accounts, Spong was a bright mind and a great public speaker—likeable and charming.

The path of Spong's beliefs tracks well with the direction of the general Episcopal Church. After over twenty years serving as rector for various churches in the mid-Atlantic, Spong was consecrated as a bishop. He proudly proclaimed himself as a contemporary Biblical scholar. In this sense, "contemporary" means that he believed that literal interpretations of the Bible were flawed. His approach calls instead for a Christianity that "must always be evolving."[25]

Thus uprooted from the text of Scriptures, Bishop Spong promoted a wide range of views contrary to two millennia of Christian faith. For example, he rejected beliefs in the Virgin Birth, the resurrection of Jesus, and in Jesus as the one and only Savior for humanity. And these were not just his private beliefs. He published widely on these subjects, with books such as *Living in Sin? A Bishop Rethinks Human Sexuality* (1988) and *Why Christianity Must Change or Die: A Bishop Speaks to Believers in Exile* (1999).

As time would show, the hot-button issue of this theological divide was sexuality. In 1994, Bishop Spong led nearly one hundred bishops to sign the "Koinonia Statement." The statement included the belief that "homosexuality and heterosexuality are morally neutral, that both can be lived out with beauty, honor, holiness, and integrity." It called for honoring those who forge same-sex partnerships. It called for honoring and protecting "the presence in the church of gay and lesbian clergy."

Bishop Spong also published open letters that he had sent to the Archbishop of Canterbury. In 1997, following the General Convention, one stated that for "the first time we have achieved a statistical majority . . . in favor of blessing same sex unions . . . the wave of the future seems clear." He wrote in another letter that "the external standards of the past, like the literal Ten Commandments and the literal Bible, can clearly no longer be held as authoritative."[26]

This was far broader than sexuality. This went to the core of what it means to be a Christian. And Spong had taken views that would long have removed him from the orthodox believers. He published "Twelve Theses" contrary to traditional faith, such as the thesis that "the view of the cross as the sacrifice for the sins of the world is a barbarian idea based on primitive concepts of God and must be dismissed." Days later a prominent Episcopal theologian responded to this thesis: "Few, if any, in the history of the Christian church have denied so much and still want to claim the name of Christian. . . . We recommend Mr. Spong resign his orders as an ordained minister of the Gospel."[27]

Spong did not. He remained a bishop in the same denomination as The Falls Church.

Sexuality and The Righter Trial

Sexuality remained the clearest indicator of the diverging beliefs. And clearer still was this litmus-test question: *are homosexual acts sinful?*

This question is revealing because it leaves no doubt as to how someone interprets the Bible. If someone interprets the text literally, then the answer is relatively easy. Many biblical passages support that the only situation in which sex is not sinful is when it is between a married man and woman.[28] The Judeo-Christian faith had not deviated from that view for two thousand years.

If someone interprets the Bible by a looser standard, a different view might arise about sexuality. Certainly, the Bible extols love. A looser interpretation suggests that the Bible's lists of certain sins were dependent on the culture of the time, and today's culture is quite different. Love is what matters most, after all. And so goes the reasoning—drifting away from literal interpretation and toward something more open-ended that could consider many expressions of sexuality to not be sinful.

This book isn't about resolving those issues. There is much more to be said about both views. They could fill books, and they have. For this story, suffice it to say that when it came to interpreting the Bible, The Falls Church consistently answered the litmus-test question above with a yes, and the Episcopal Church began to answer it with a no.

As Yates had preached in his first years at The Falls Church, healthy sexuality was central to good marriages and new life. As early as June 1981, he noted the divided opinion of Americans on abortion and homosexuality. The context for his point was that "the authority of Christ demands similarly the authority of scripture in our lives. There is no way around this as Christians. We Christians are not our own authority. We are men and women under authority. Therefore, while it is very interesting to keep up with the moral opinions of people around us, to understand what other people believe, our ultimate responsibility is to ask ourselves, 'Yes, but what does Christ say about it? What does the Holy Word of God teach us to believe about it?'"[29]

Yates also warned against watering down religion to make it "attractive and popular" to people. "It is not, however, our job to alter Christianity to suit people, but to alter people to suit Christianity."

Yates made clear that this included sexuality. "From beginning to end, the Scripture is very clear that any kind of sexual involvement outside the bonds of marriage is sin. . . . In fact, our Lord even went so far as to say that if in your own heart and mind you give careful thought to such a relationship, it is sin as well. This does not just apply to people within the bonds of marriage. It applies to everyone."[30]

Simply put, Yates and most at The Falls Church believed in the primacy of Scripture and its teaching on sexuality. But obviously, and as subsequent decades have shown, cultural views on this issue have changed.

The change did not happen overnight within the Episcopal Church. The story of Bishop Righter makes this clear. He had been the bishop of Iowa from 1972 to 1988. During that time, Righter had written that homosexuality was an illness that could be cured. He also voted against the ordination of homosexuals in 1979.[31] In 1989, after retiring, he moved to New Jersey to serve as assistant bishop to Bishop Spong. Like many who heard Bishop Spong's message, Righter changed his views. In 1990, he ordained an openly gay rector who was living with his partner. He signed the Koinonia Statement in support of ordaining noncelibate homosexuals.

This did not go down easily with church leadership, either locally or nationally. Things came to a head in 1995, when ten Episcopal bishops brought formal accusations against Bishop Righter. One-fourth of the church's 300 bishops supported this accusation. They held a hearing on February 27, 1996, in Delaware.

Hugo Blankingship, a member of The Falls Church, found himself as the attorney representing the ten bishops bringing the charge. He'd agreed to support the lead attorney, Bishop Wantland of Wisconsin, but Wantland was required to recuse because he "might be called as witness." Blankingship laughs at the memory now. It was not a strong ground to disqualify Wantland, especially when four of the bishops hearing the case had already ordained practicing gay priests. "We requested that they recuse, too, but they wouldn't," Blankingship said.

"So I went up to the cathedral in Wilmington for the hearing. It was an all-day argument, and the room was full. So was the spillover room. The bishops bombarded me with questions. The other side made their argument."

The hearing focused on a single, threshold question: was there a doctrine—any view at all—in the Episcopal Church on ordaining practicing gay priests. Seven of the eight bishops voted no. Their conclusion was that "the Episcopal Church has no core doctrine [that is, no foundational teaching] in the area of human sexuality, and therefore neither the doctrine nor the discipline of the Church has been violated in this ordination."

The case against Bishop Righter was dismissed.

The Righter trial was not a one-off event. "It opened the floodgates," recalls one Falls Church member. At the time, this member served on a discernment committee for an Episcopal priest's potential ordination in Washington, D.C. The committee met with Bishop Jane Dixon, the second female bishop in the Episcopal Church. "I don't recall the exact question posed to Bishop Dixon," the member said, "but I have not forgotten her response: She exclaimed that she wanted to see a homosexual priest placed in every parish in the Diocese. A few others on the discernment committee looked as incredulous as I, but the majority acquiesced to approval of that position."

With such changes gaining pace after the Righter trial, many members of the Falls Church vestry were ready to leave the Episcopal denomination. Yates was not.

"No," he said, definitively.

He explained that the church's focus needed to be on trying to bring about change *within* the Episcopal Church. That did not mean that Yates agreed with the Episcopal Church's views on sexuality or any of the larger issues. At the vestry's request, on July 14, 1996, he preached an entire sermon on "the disturbing things now going on in the life of the Episcopal Church."

Yates explained that, in some ways, the Episcopal Church was better than it had been. Instead of "traditional, comfortable, quiet," and "pretty dull," the late 1960s and 1970s witnessed a revival among young people. It was "a wind of spiritual uplift" blowing through the church, bringing people to life in Christ and rediscovery of the Bible. But since then, Yates explained, the Episcopal Church had split into "two theological camps"—orthodox and revisionist. A major divide between these camps was whether the Scripture was God's true, authoritative word or subject to change based on culture.

Yates explained how rigorous the process for selecting bishops was, and how the ordination of non-celibate same-sex individuals had become "the heart of the debate." He reviewed what the Bible says about sex and reaffirmed his view that sex is only proper between a husband and wife. He added, "There is absolutely nothing in Holy Scripture to support any goodness of homosexual practices." He then put the conclusion of the Righter trial in clear terms: "In one sentence, those seven bishops rejected two thousand years of the Church's teaching and four thousand years of careful effort on the part of Jews and Christians to obey the Scriptural teaching on sexual morality."

But as always, it wasn't just about sexuality. Yates made clear that "we don't single out this one sin as worse than others. God condemns all sin, whether it be arrogance or murder or slander or selfishness or idolatry or slavery or theft, or whatever it is. And, we certainly don't say that persons who are committing sin can't come to church. For heaven's sake, of one thing we're certain: we're all sinners. All of us break God's laws; none of us keep his standards completely. We are the fellowship of the sinful, but we are the fellowship of repenting, repentant, and forgiven sinners."

He said that the church was called to "do everything we can to support and help them. And we are called to love those who are even willfully breaking God's commandments. God loves them as much as he loves you and me but we don't approve. We accept them, but we don't accept their lifestyle. We don't approve of their lifestyle, but neither do we condemn them. No. We weep for them, we pray for them—just as we weep for anyone who has not yet come to embrace the way of the Lord—because, and this is so important, only in a life of personal purity and holiness will a person find God's deepest secrets. Only in a life of personal purity and holiness will a person enjoy genuine intimacy with the Holy Spirit. The only vessel that God will fill is the one that God has emptied and cleansed."

Yates concluded with great concern for the schism in the church. "A Church that would allow itself to be pressured into accepting homosexual practices or partnerships, or into approving sex outside of marriage between a man and a woman, would be a church that has departed from Scripture and is in opposition to the Holy Spirit."[32]

The Growing Global Rift

Other Episcopal leaders were taking strong stances against the changing sexual mores. Charles Murphy and others issued the "First Promise" statement, which directly confronted church leadership and laid out principles in conflict with the Koinonia Statement. It declared the authority of the Episcopal Church to be "fundamentally impaired," and its signers indicated that they would "be in communion with that part of the Anglican Communion which accepts and endorses the principles aforesaid and not otherwise." In other words, they would leave the Episcopal Church if it did not change. There were immediate ramifications as well. The signers vowed to "not fund, nor recommend funding, any legal institution, organization or person whose actions aid or further teach" contrary to God's written Word.

John Yates did not sign the First Promise statement. While he agreed with the moral principles, he thought it went too far in the direction of disrespect or insubordination. Only one Anglican bishop—John Rucyahana from Rwanda—signed the statement.[33] But that did not mean that the Anglican Communion approved of the Episcopal Church's changing practices on sexuality.

Another effort for change within the Episcopal Church was a new organization called the American Anglican Council (AAC). A member of The Falls Church helped prepare the by-laws for the council, and the church's senior wardens served at different times on the national board. The AAC publicly expressed concern about the Episcopal Church's leadership moving "further and further away from the historic biblical Christian faith, as if locked in a downward spiraling dance of death with the postmodern Western culture."[34]

In 1997, at the Episcopal Church's triennial General Convention, there was a resolution proposed on a "Statement on Human Sexuality." Bishops of the southern hemisphere had developed the resolution, which read in part: "The Holy Scriptures are clear in teaching that all sexual promiscuity is sin. We are convinced that this includes homosexual practices between men or women, as well as heterosexual relationships outside marriage." The Episcopal Bishops voted against the resolution 94-42.

The convention also included election of a new presiding bishop, Frank Griswold, who had previously ordained non-celibate homosexuals and encouraged the blessing of same-gender unions. In an interview in late 1997, Griswold stated:

Broadly speaking, the Episcopal Church is in conflict with Scripture. The only way to justify it is to say, well, Jesus talks about the Spirit guiding the church and guiding believers and bringing to their awareness things they cannot deal with yet. So one would have to say that the mind of Christ operative in the church over time . . . has led the church to, in effect, contradict the words of the Gospel.[35]

Meanwhile, in the broader Anglican Communion, the time had come for the Lambeth Conference. This gathering of the church's leaders from around the world happened every ten years. It came as no surprise that the discussion centered on sexuality. The church leaders, by a 526 to 70 vote, passed a resolution calling for a "listening process" on homosexuality, but also declaring "homosexual practice as incompatible with the Scripture."

Bishop Spong called the actions of this Lambeth Conference "strange" and "almost pathological." He added: "The winning resolution revealed an attitude toward Holy Scripture that reflected total ignorance of the last 100 years of critical biblical scholarship. It also revealed an absolute void in knowledge of contemporary medical and scientific data in regard to the origins and nature of homosexual orientation . . . Let me say this carefully, but clearly. Anyone who elevates their prejudices to the position where they are defended as the will of God is evil."[36]

With "evil" so evoked, Bishop Spong eliminated any potential doubt: this was not just a political struggle, it was a spiritual one. In the summer of 2000, such heated rhetoric filled the air at the next General Convention of the Episcopal Church. The Convention passed by overwhelming majority a resolution that formally accepted couples "who are living in other [non-marital] life-long committed relationships."[37] The divide between the Episcopal Church's leadership and the Anglican Communion's leadership could not have been clearer.

After the General Convention in 2000, several churches left the Episcopal Church. A congregation in Littleton, Colorado walked away from their new church building. Congregations in Destin, Florida and Mobile, Alabama also voted to leave and lost their properties to the Episcopal Church. Many clergy who led these churches were defrocked, and they joined Anglican provinces from Africa.

Leaders of the Anglican Communion in the global South continued to express strong disapproval of the changing views of the Episcopal Church. In 2000, Archbishop Kolini of Rwanda and Archbishop Tay of Southeast Asia took a bold step. They met in Singapore to consecrate two American Episcopal clergyman as bishops of foreign provinces. They commissioned these two men—Chuck Murphy and John Rodgers—"to minister to the United States of

America." This initiative "aimed at reversing a 30-year decline of 30 percent in the membership of the Episcopal Church," as part of "an ongoing effort to lead the Episcopal Church back to its biblical foundations." In other words, Anglican leaders in the global South were sending missionaries to America.[38]

One notable participant in this consecration was Bishop C. FitzSimons Allison of South Carolina. Not only was Bishop Allison one of the few Americans willing to take this controversial step against the Episcopal Church, he was also Susan Yates's uncle. As Susan said, "Uncle Fitz led the way." This bold step by a family member, despite clear risks, became an encouragement to the Yates.

Yet some Anglican leaders bristled at the consecrations in Singapore. They believed that such territorial intrusions were irregular and went against church tradition. A prominent theologian, N.T. Wright, explained: "border crossings are disruptive. Not only are they against the spirit and letter of Anglican formularies, they are against one of the [church fathers'] decrees of the Council of Nicea."[39]

The disagreement gave rise to even harsher words by Episcopal leaders. As usual, Bishop Spong put it in stark terms. He described the ordination of these two bishops as "a power grab by an antiquated minority." One archbishop, Rowan Williams, who would later become the Archbishop of Canterbury, commented on the consecrations in the global South and described the stakes well: "The theological fireworks of Bishop John Spong . . . who has been cutting long swathes through pretty well every received doctrine and ethical conviction of classical Christianity, have done a lot to sharpen up this discontent. Has North American Anglicanism no means at all, people ask, of reining in pluralism? And if it hasn't, are its structures at all trustworthy?"[40]

The Falls Church As A Light

The Falls Church remained steady in its views. It issued a statement making clear its position on sexuality. Soon after the Righter trial, the vestry at The Falls Church changed the church's donations so that members would be able to indicate whether or not they wanted a portion of their pledges to go to the Episcopal Church. Only 16% wanted to support the denomination with their contributions.

While church funds were segregated starting in the late 1990s, John Yates and The Falls Church were making no moves toward leaving the Episcopal Church.

Yates did not want to leave the Episcopal Church. His calling was to work for renewal within the church, not to break away from it. He did not want division. One Sunday in early 1996 he recounted how evangelism had led to many differences across churches. "Church changes in different contexts, and that's not bad. The truths of God never change, but, as we move from one culture or one setting to another, many of our church customs will change."

These changes, Yates explained, led to questions about what was essential to the Christian faith. There was much room for disagreement, but one thing had to be clear:

> In every church, and in every generation, believers must reaffirm one thing over and over again, and that's this: God offers to all people his love, himself, eternal life in heaven with him through the means of faith in Christ, and him alone. There's no room for disagreement on this. . . . There's only one way to eternal life with God. It's not living a good life. It's not being spiritual. It's not Mohammed or Buddha. It's the heart of our doctrine.

Yates then turned the attention to division. He gave the example of Paul and Barnabas disagreeing in Acts.

Dear friends, whether it's in your home, or your church, your marriage or your family, in your relationship between friends, work for unity. Avoid quarrelsomeness; avoid divisiveness; avoid it like the plague. Dissension is of the devil. It divides God's people. Follow the example of the apostles here in the first council. Come together; listen; share your experiences; share your understanding of Scripture; pray; seek the guidance of the Holy Spirit; and then come to a decision. Affirm your desire simply to obey Christ. Don't allow for sinful division. When there's disagreement, well, continue to love and serve and support those you can't agree with.[41]

The Falls Church was a bulwark of orthodox faith, and it continued to attract new members. When newcomers visited, like so many before, they felt as if the preaching hit home—speaking directly into their lives. The congregation again filled its available space. Years earlier the church had a big vision when it funded and built the new sanctuary. But even that larger space had reached capacity. By the early 2000s, the church was offering multiple services—even using various locations at the same time—to try to fit everyone. Again people were turned away at the doors for lack of seats.

The church had acquired a property across the street, known as Southgate. It included a parking lot and a strip-mall style building. The church hired engineers who developed plans for an immense family center. It would have included meeting spaces and a full gymnasium. The cost estimates reached $28 million.

It didn't happen. The plans hit obstacle after obstacle. All the tenants on the new property left—all except for a Kurdish restaurant that hadn't paid rent in three years. It threatened litigation. The city also had objections to the plans. They didn't want to close the street that ran between the church and the planned building. The church considered building a bridge over the road. Cost projections continued to rise.

"It died a natural death," said the senior warden at the time, Howard Shafferman. "I was secretly relieved."

In hindsight, it may have been God's protection that kept The Falls Church from investing more in that location. Major property trouble loomed on the horizon.

10

The Breaking Point

We began to hear our leaders losing confidence in the uniqueness of the person of Jesus Christ. The denomination was turning away from the Word of God, as its authority. When a church loses confidence in the Scriptures, that church loses its vitality, it loses its reason for being. That's what happened in the denomination.

John Yates

On October 31, 1517, a German man bundled a thick document under his arm. He walked from his home to a church. He passed under a gothic arch and faced the wide double door beneath it. He pulled a hammer and nail from his cloak. He began to hammer the document onto the aged wooden surface. He slammed the nail all the way in, pinning the pages there for all to see.

The man, of course, was Martin Luther. The church was All Saints' Church, a Catholic cathedral in Wittenberg, Saxony. Luther's nailing of the Ninety-Five theses to the door changed the course of religious history.

But did that document—that hammer and nail—start the Reformation by itself?

The Ninety-Five Theses on the Power and Efficacy of Indulgences protested many practices of the Catholic Church, from nepotism to the sale of indulgences. Those practices had been going on for years, and they were intensifying. Nailing the theses was the trigger of events to come, but the stage had been set many years before.

So it was with the conflict inside the Episcopal Church. The

93

ordination of a gay bishop was a trigger. It was the surface event that exposed deep rifts about what it means to be a Christian. Those rifts had been growing for years, and the slow drift might have continued if not for a trigger. Sometimes it takes a trigger to force hard decisions.

The First Gay Bishop

Gene Robinson became a priest in the Episcopal Church in 1973. He moved to New Hampshire with his wife of several years, and they settled down and had two children. In 1986, he and his wife divorced. Two years later he entered a relationship with another man. He worked closely with the bishop of New Hampshire in the following years, and in 2003, he was elected bishop coadjutor (the second-in-command and successor bishop) of the region.

For procedural reasons, Robinson's election presented the first opportunity for the Episcopal General Convention to vote yes or no about a practicing gay bishop. These triennial conventions have hundreds of attendees—"seductively magnificent and grand affairs," as one attendee put it. There are votes by bishops, by clergy, and by lay members.

The fateful vote about Bishop Robinson took place in Minneapolis, Minnesota in August 2003. George Hooper, a Falls Church vestryman, attended the Convention. "No one expected anything less than a further splitting of the two sides," he said. He watched closely as the Episcopal bishops battled over confirming Robinson's elevation to bishop. "I heard one group claim that his selection 'was the Holy Spirit revealing new truths to us,' while the other side warned that 'approval of this will tear the fabric of the Anglican Communion at its deepest level.'" George found the experience deeply disheartening. He vowed that this Convention—his fourth in a row—would be his last.

After much debate and discussion, the bishop, clergy, and lay members' voting groups approved the election of Gene Robinson.

Each segment had roughly 60 percent approval—a significant majority.

One person's "yes" vote shocked The Falls Church. The church's leadership had long been good friends with Peter Lee, the Bishop of the Diocese of Virginia. Bishop Lee had been holding his cards close to his chest for years. He favored unity and tolerance, but he never indicated a clear position on issues of sexuality. The vote on Bishop Robinson forced clarity, and Bishop Lee—who had a measure of authority over The Falls Church—went with prevailing currents. The church had lost an important ally.

In case any doubts remained about Bishop Lee's position, he made clear once and for all his main priority. On January 31, 2004, before a gathering of over 500 Episcopalians in Virginia, he said, "If you must make a choice between heresy and schism, always choose heresy."[42]

This statement, as one Falls Church member said, "was the bursting of the boil." The difference seemed impossible to overcome.

And this showed more was at stake than just sexuality. At the same national General Convention where the Episcopal Church affirmed the ordination of Gene Robinson, the bishops voted to reject a resolution that would have reaffirmed "Holy Scripture as the foundation of authority in our Church." At least the bishops were consistent. The Bible was out, Robinson was in.

Thirty Years At Sea

Even before joining The Falls Church in 1979, John Yates's calling and his passion had been renewal of the Episcopal Church. He worked at this in the 1970s. He worked at it in the 1980s and 1990s.

In 2003, while the Episcopal General Convention was underway, Yates was away on a three-month sabbatical. He happened to be in Vancouver, visiting his son and friends there, when the vote about Gene Robinson took place. This distance helped him look at his thirty years of renewal work with a different perspective.

Yates's early vision of the Falls Church was of a ship stuck in the ice. He lit the fires around its perimeter. By the power of the Holy Spirit, he helped get the ship unstuck and going in a new direction. Many people joined him. The church grew from a couple hundred to several thousand. In many ways, he had sparked renewal at The Falls Church.

But the Episcopal Church was a different ship entirely. On sabbatical, Yates came to see the denomination as a huge rusty ocean liner. Heresy was making it unseaworthy. Its captain and top officers were untrustworthy. They couldn't seem to see that the ship was sinking. Anglican leaders from the global South captained smaller, more nimble vessels. They pulled their little boats alongside the ocean liner, and people were beginning to jump off the sinking ship for these more reliable vessels.[43] It had become unbearable to bear the name "Episcopal" when it was openly committed to error and was never turning back.

Yates returned from sabbatical with a new approach. For the first time in three decades, his focus was no longer renewal within the Episcopal Church. He had led the amazing renewal of *an* Episcopal church, but the broader denomination was sinking.

A friend said to him, "You've changed, haven't you?"

"We've been forced to change," Yates replied.

Yates met with the senior warden at the time, Rich Dean, and told him The Falls Church needed to change its strategy. He asked Rich to help by staying on as the senior warden for another term—the only time he has ever made such a request.

"I didn't want to change who was in the saddle," Yates explained. "We needed Rich. He has broad shoulders, and not just because he's a former Vanderbilt football player. He'd spent his life in the Scriptures. He was as unflappable as anyone I've ever known."

Rich Dean had started attending The Falls Church in the early 1990s. He loved the youth program and the preaching. It wasn't long before he was on the vestry. He served until the time of the Righter trial in 1996.

"In those years," Rich recalled, "the vestry was often pulling John Yates along with it on the controversial issues. There was no talk of leaving. There probably wouldn't have been if things had stayed on the same path."

But things didn't. The Episcopal Church continued to evolve away from The Falls Church and others like it. Rich returned to the vestry in 2000 and became the senior warden. In 2003, after Gene Robinson's ordination, The Falls Church began preparing to leave the Episcopal Church. Rich agreed to stay on as senior warden. He smiled at the memory. "This time it was the vestry holding John back." The focus shifted to creating a new Anglican church in North America.

The reason was not sexuality. Although the Bishop Righter trial and Bishop Robinson's election had put the topic in the limelight, it was about something deeper. It was about the belief that the Scriptures were true. Yates had confirmed his own belief years before, and he explained this to the church soon after his return from sabbatical:

> Over the last two generations, our denomination has tolerated leaders and teachers who have jettisoned historic doctrines of the Church—many believers have left the church in disgust. We have stayed.
>
> Now a General Convention decision has clarified starkly for all of us that the Episcopal Church has moved even further away from Scripture. Ninety-two bishops, a devastating majority, refused to endorse a resolution reaffirming Holy Scripture as the foundation of authority in our church, reaffirming the historic statements of Anglicanism concerning scripture. It is clear, we have to say, *Enough* . . . we can go no further, and so we have appealed to the Archbishop of Canterbury and the Primates, and they have intervened on behalf of biblical truth.
>
> The ultimate issue is one of authority—it is that of lordship of Christ. *You call me teacher and Lord,* he said, *and rightly so. For that is what I am.* We have no liberty to disobey or disagree with

him. We bow to the authority and total trustworthiness of scripture because we bow to the authority of Christ.[44]

A week later, Yates made clear how this primacy of Christ and scripture affected the ongoing sexuality debate. He told the church about how, for the preceding six years, he had accepted Bishop Lee's request to participate in a group of fifteen to twenty Episcopalians "of every conceivable persuasion" to talk about sexuality. "I have made some friends," Yates said. "I have come to appreciate many different points of view. I have listened to people describe their experiences. But, in this group I cannot recall ever taking the time to look together at God's word to see what God himself says about sexuality."

That was the central problem. Not Bishop Righter, not Bishop Robinson, not sexuality itself—but belief in the word of God. "What we have been doing in the Episcopal Church is elevating the authority of individual experience and, at the same time, neglecting the thoughtful study of Scripture. As a result, people have become their own authority. When we turn away from the Scriptures, we will be shaped and directed by who can tell the most moving stories, those whose experiences touch us most deeply."

With those fateful words, Yates seemed to forecast the path of the same-sex marriage movement in the decade to come. The proponents told the most moving stories, and those stories prevailed upon a culture to change. Those who put the Scripture first, however, had reached a line they could not cross.

Yates knew the important questions the church faced. He did not shy away from them, and instead put them clearly before the congregation: "How can we disassociate ourselves from what the Episcopal Church has done, and has become, without disconnecting from the faithful? How can we be godly stewards of our historic property and facilities and funds? How can we be faithful to the vision God has given us?"

The members of The Falls Church were divided on these questions. Some people wanted to wait and watch—to not take action.

Others yearned for bold action. They would have the church leave its property and strike out on its own. Yates described the middle ground that the church would come to agree upon.

> Most think that the way of the Lord is toward the establishment of a new thing, a new realignment of orthodox churches, with faithful bishops aligned—not with unrepentant Episcopal leadership but with the wider Anglican family. We don't want to be an independent church; we want to be a biblical Anglican church. We don't want to rebel against authority, we want godly authority. Godly authority now is coming out of the south: Africa, South America, and Asia. It's not perfect, but the instincts of these men and women have not been so tainted by modernism as to have set themselves above Scripture.
>
> You know, our children are going to be confused enough already growing up in this secular, materialistic culture that we live in here and now, but to be in a church that blesses immorality when we could be in a godly Anglican network, I think the way begins to become clear. I look at my grandchildren, and I know that the time has come to move in a different direction toward some kind of a new alignment, not geographically based, but organized around the mission, the Great Commission rooted in Scripture. . . .
>
> We don't need to be in a hurry. We pray, we listen, we confer with other trusted leaders elsewhere. And as wisely as possible, we lay out plans, realizing there are many unknowns. And finally, we commit to a course of action, and we give responsibility to the best persons for leadership and we proceed to implement those decisions relying upon the Holy Spirit. We communicate to the whole church family in writing and in person. We depend upon the Spirit to correct, to confirm, to carry forward. That's the way a group of Christian people seek to discern the way of Christ, and every step is important.

Three Years of Negotiation

John Yates and The Falls Church were not the only ones with a new focus—who had said, "Enough." Bishop Robinson's election had drawn a clear and impassable battle line. But that did not have to mean war among Christians. Believers are called to resolve their conflicts peaceably, out of the courts. That's what they tried to do, both locally and more broadly.

These efforts rose to the highest level of the Anglican Communion. The Communion has thirty-eight regional provinces, each headed by an archbishop or presiding bishop. The provinces are autonomous, and their leaders gather to discuss matters of the broader Communion. There is no official mechanism for one province to impose its views on another province. But the greatest influence has long resided with the Archbishop of Canterbury. He is the figurehead, often serving as the peacemaker.

In 2003, the Archbishop of Canterbury, Rowan Williams, called a special meeting of the leaders of the Anglican Communion—the most senior bishops in each of the Communion's provinces. These international leaders, known as Primates, stated that Robinson's election "threaten[ed] the unity of our Communion as well as our relationships with other parts of Christ's Church, our mission and witness, and our relations with other faiths, in a world already confused in areas of sexuality, morality and theology, and polarize[d] Christian opinion."

Archbishop Williams also established a commission—the Lambeth Commission—to study these issues. The Commission issued the Windsor Report in October 2004. The report noted the intense and divisive issue of human sexuality. It described the consent to Bishop Robinson's election and similar moves as having "uncovered major divisions throughout the Anglican Communion. There has been talk of crisis, schism and realignment. Voices and declarations have portrayed a Communion in crisis." The report added: "The depth of conviction and feeling on all sides of the current issues has on occasions introduced a degree of harshness and a lack of charity which is new to Anglicanism. A process of dissent is not new to the Communion but it has never before been expressed with such force nor in ways which have been so accessible to international scrutiny."

The Windsor Report recommended that the Episcopal Church "be invited to express its regret that the proper constraints of the bonds of affection were breached in the events surrounding the election and consecration of a bishop for the See of New Hampshire," and that "pending such expression of regret, those who took part as consecrators of Gene Robinson should be invited to consider in all conscience whether they should withdraw themselves from representative functions in the Anglican Communion."

While the report warned of needing to "walk apart" and was generally critical of the actions of the Episcopal Church, the tone was diplomatic—too diplomatic, according to some.

The Primate for Nigeria, Peter Akinola, wrote that the report "fails to confront the reality that a small economically privileged group of people has sought to subvert the Christian faith and impose their new and false doctrine on the wider community of faithful believers. We have watched in sadness as sisters and brothers who have sought to maintain their allegiance to the 'faith once delivered to the saints' have been marginalized and persecuted for their faith. We have been filled with grief as we have witnessed the decline of the North American Church."

The Church of Nigeria continued to lead in pivotal steps away from the Episcopal Church, the traditional arm of the Anglican Communion in the United States. It refused to accept financial contributions from the Episcopal Church, and it ceased their prior exchange of bishops. The Church of Nigeria also revised its structure and established the Convocation of Anglican Nigerians in America (CANA), removing geographic barriers so that churches located in

North America could join an African branch. This unprecedented division was for the spiritual care of Nigerian Anglicans in America.

CANA soon changed its name for a broader purpose. It became the Convocation of Anglicans in North America. As one article put it, "the Nigerian outreach to America officially began, on the fertile mission fields of Northern Virginia. And the natives here are restless."[45]

An early leader of CANA was Martyn Minns, who had been ordained by the Church of Nigeria as a bishop and missionary to congregations in America. Minns hardly fit expectations of an African missionary. He was a tall, British, former Mobil Oil executive. After he entered ministry, he served at a renewed, charismatic Episcopal church in Darien, Connecticut in the 1970s—the same church mentioned earlier in this book as the place where Terry Fullam had warned about the Episcopal decline and need for renewal. Minns caught that fire of renewal. He came to lead the thriving Truro Church in Fairfax, Virginia, often with a tambourine in his hand.

Minns described this Anglican realignment as a "flat" church: the "new congregations are breaking out of their hierarchical straightjackets and connecting directly with other parts of the Anglican Communion. What unites them is a vision for global Christianity; a commitment to a common language of faith and abiding friendships that connect across challenging cultural divides."[46] And so Minns became a bishop from Nigeria—ready to help churches like The Falls Church in the days ahead.

A Virginia Way?

In 2004, Bishop Lee led the Virginia diocese to establish a "Reconciliation Commission" of thirteen church leaders. The commission studied the divisive issues and, in January 2005, published a report considering the possibility of an "amicable divorce." The commission noted that it wasn't just about sexuality, but that there were "larger issues of the interpretation of scripture, the apostolic tradition, and the relationship of the Episcopal Church with the Anglican Communion. In the context of our apostolic tradition and our relationship with the Anglican Communion, these differences have led to genuine pain, fear, confusion, and impaired communion."[47]

Within The Falls Church, the vestry decided the same year that it would no longer give money to the Episcopal Church. Members of the congregation could still contribute directly to the Episcopal Church if they wished.

Later that year, Bishop Lee wrote to the national presiding bishop with concern about Virginia parishes. He said he'd received hundreds of negative letters and notices that parishes were ensuring they provided no financial support to the Episcopal denomination. The lawyer for the church's head bishop began planning for rifts in the church. The same day, Bishop Lee also wrote to the Archbishop of Canterbury. He encouraged the Archbishop not to support efforts at division, and said "you are in my daily prayers as you wrestle with this fractious Communion."[48]

On September 27, 2005, Yates wrote to Bishop Lee. "Here is the pressure: If it becomes clear that [the Episcopal Church] will not turn back on this issue, we are pained to say that we believe we will have to find a way to separate from [the Episcopal Church], while remaining Anglicans. We have no plan, no timetable of action. Our great hope is that here in Virginia there may be an opportunity to forge a better way, perhaps a middle way. This has always been your hallmark. What such a plan might look like I do not care to speculate about, but we would very much like to pursue with you and any whom you would designate as your representatives, just how we might achieve what could be seen to be a win-win solution. Our people are extremely upset. We have all lost key church members and more are leaving all the time. We don't know how long we can hold together."

Bishop Lee agreed to meet with twenty-five clergymen from Virginia to discuss this. Bishop Lee heard, in person, how upset people were.

"I don't think we'll be able to remain," one rector said.

Another asked Bishop Lee, "Will you work with us so we can leave peacefully?"

Bishop Lee agreed. They would try "a Virginia approach"—genteel and gracious.

The first step was Bishop Lee's appointment of a committee. It included Yates and five others—three on each side of the issues. "It was a sweet-spirited group—the peacemakers," Yates recalled. They met once a month for a year. The issue of church property loomed over the discussions.

After much deliberation and compromise, on September 28, 2006—almost exactly one year after Yates's letter to Bishop Lee—the committee decided on protocols for parishes that wanted to leave the Episcopal Church. The protocols included thirty days of discernment, a 70 percent vote by the congregation, and approval by the Bishops' Standing Committee and the executive committee. The committee's report stated: "We candidly and regretfully acknowledge that we may be entering a period in the history of the Anglican Communion when we (the Church, the Body of Christ) will be walking the way of the Cross together, but apart."

Bishop Lee did not necessarily like this, but he agreed to it. All the elements were in place for a peaceable separation. But an unfortunate surprise awaited.

11

New Sheriff In Town

For certain people have crept in unnoticed
who long ago were designated for this condemnation,
ungodly people, who pervert the grace of our God into sensuality
and deny our only Master and Lord, Jesus Christ.
Jude 1:4

While The Falls Church and many others in Virginia worked toward a peaceable separation in 2006, the Episcopal Church held another General Convention. Many important issues were on the agenda. Schisms in the church were deep. Someone proposed a resolution declaring the church's belief that salvation was through Christ alone, "the only name by which any person may be saved." The committee considering the resolution rejected it by a 70-percent majority.[49]

At the 2006 convention, the church faced another significant question: who would be its next leader?

The presiding bishop of the Episcopal Church typically serves in that capacity for twelve years. Frank Griswold had held this position in the prior years of controversy. His approach had been one of accommodation, including tolerance of clear deviation by Episcopal bishops from the Lambeth resolutions of 1998 affirming traditional church views on sexuality. Griswold himself, when he previously served as a bishop in Chicago, had ordained practicing homosexuals. He sympathized with the pressure in local communities for this change. But mainly, he was not willing to act as an enforcer of any view. He told a delegation of African bishops that he held an "honorary office." That meant he "presided over autonomous bishops and dioceses who have the right to do what they want to do."[50]

Seven candidates vied to succeed Frank Griswold as presiding bishop. Six of the candidates were males from Southern dioceses. One candidate was a female from Nevada. She had served in ministry for the shortest period of time among the candidates. Her name was Katharine Jefferts Schori. She became the first woman elected as a Primate in the Anglican Communion.

Bishop Schori's election was no coincidence. Generally, Christians do not believe in coincidence. All things happen according to God's plan, in ways humans cannot understand. But not all things that happen are good, because not all forces are good. God has an enemy in the devil. The Bible tells the story of Job, a rich man who lost his wealth, his home, his family—everything he cared about. It was the devil who came to God and asked to harass Job. God gave the devil permission to do it, so that Job could demonstrate his commitment to God despite his circumstances, and that God could bless him richly for it.

The massive division of a church is exactly where forces of good and evil would meet. It is exactly where spiritual battles affect reality, even if beyond human sight. People can sense such epic turmoil, and with Bishop Schori, there was a clear sense of darkness at work. "When Bishop Schori came," Jean Trakowski recalls, "there was a feeling of great horror."

The tone of the division changed. It was no longer an amicable divorce. It was headed towards court.

The End of Negotiation

John Yates had the Virginia protocol in hand. With Bishop Lee's consent, the procedures were in place for a vote and a peaceable separation. The congregation had devoted months to focused prayer, Bible study, and discussion about the situation. Representatives from the Diocese of Virginia had been invited to come and express their opinions to the congregation. The church was informed and deeply involved. The vote was scheduled for Sunday, December 10, 2006.

The week before the vote, Bishop Lee met with John and informed him: "Everything is off."

John was shocked. "What?"

"It's all over now," Bishop Lee said. "No church will be able to keep its property."

John did not understand. Even the presiding bishop did not have this kind of authority, but Bishop Lee wasn't one to boldly resist the influence of leadership. He would not budge.

"There's a new sheriff in town," the Bishop told John. "The situation is different."

Presiding Bishop Schori and the Executive Council of the Episcopal Church had adopted a new policy. The former Presiding Bishop Griswold had said that the national church would become involved in parish property disputes only if invited by the local bishop and diocesan standing committees. In other words, if local churches could resolve their differences amicably, then national Episcopal leaders would not stand in the way. But starting in December 2006, Bishop Schori led the Episcopal Church to adopt an unprecedented, categorical rule. The church would prohibit any negotiation over the transfer of property to departing congregations.

Bishop Lee played the role of messenger, applying this policy for Virginia churches. On December 1, 2006, he wrote with a clear warning: "absent a negotiated settlement of property, an attempt to place your congregation and its real and personal property under the authority of any ecclesial body other than the Diocese of Virginia and the bodies authorized by its canons to hold church property will have repercussions and possible civil liability for individual vestry members."[51]

This threat was personal. It threw down the gauntlet for vestry members—would they lead The Falls Church to a vote in the face of personal, financial losses? In response, one vestry member emailed another with a picture of several of his children holding a sign that read, "Evicted by bishop, will work for food." This was funny, but it was not simply light-hearted. These leaders knew the stakes, and they knew about Christ's suffering. They counted it as joy to stand for truth and to have this small chance to share in His suffering.

Still, it was not easy as The Falls Church proceeded to its vote on December 10. A few vestry members pushed to stay in the Episcopal Church and continue working for good from within, while another had a vivid dream of getting out of the building before it collapsed. The church's senior warden, Tom Wilson, gracefully managed the discussions, ensuring every vestry member's voice was heard. Clergyman Rick Wright provided quiet leadership behind the scenes. In the end, they recommended to the congregation that it vote to leave.

This recommendation did not mitigate the risk of losing the property. Many in the congregation feared this. "I knew we were going to lose it," said one member. "I never had a doubt in my mind." The local press fueled these concerns, reporting that "the stage is set for what could be a monumental battle over control of the historic church properties," with a value "estimated at $27 million, but could be much higher . . . ."[52]

Others were far less sure. "We built this church," another member said. "People knew in the back of their minds that it was possible we could lose the property, but that wasn't the main concern."

Whatever the risk posed to the property, this vote was about the church's faith, and more. These people had been together, soaked in the Word of God, filled with the Holy Spirit, and shepherded by John Yates—some for over two decades. Looking back, it's not hard to imagine that God was preparing them for this difficult time. Their beliefs had been shaped deep in their souls, and now it was time to act on them.

They also were not thinking simply of themselves. They were thinking of the church's witness to others. As Yates said, "This whole situation in which we find ourselves as a church, it's not about us. It's about those children, the next generation, and the next generation, and the next generation. It's about passing down the truth of God to them. Friends, for the sake of the children, we must be people of truth and people of grace."[53]

Mark and Katherine Weller remember sitting down with their kids on the day of the vote. "This was about the inerrancy of scripture," Katherine said, "and we wanted our kids to know that. We gave them an example. We're all taught that $2 + 2 = 4$. Well, this is like someone changing that and telling you: '$2 + 2 = 4$ . . . or maybe 5 . . . depending on your preference.' We wanted our kids to know that we were voting to leave because we still believed that $2 + 2 = 4$."

The senior generation also played a powerful role. Susan Yates remembers the encouragement from these "older saints"—those who are not traditionally the risk-takers. At one of the meetings discussing whether to leave, a white-haired woman stood and said, "I'm 95 years old, and we have to stand for truth. We have to leave."

Another couple—Allen and Frances Long—showed that this was not about casting aside commitments. The Longs had known each other eighty years, and they'd been married for the last sixty. They started attending The Falls Church in 1958. They served the church in many capacities. But by the time Allen turned ninety, he had suffered several strokes. Allen still smiled wide and shook hands firmly. He could not get many words out, but Frances understood him. They communicated in winks and laughs. Six decades of committed marriage gave them their own language.

Frances loved talking about her family. Warm, honest, and matter-of-fact—she's the kind of great-grandmother we all want to have. In 1969, she was the church's first female delegate to the annual meeting of the Episcopal Diocese. No one could question this woman's loyalty.

When asked if it was difficult to leave the Episcopal Church after all those years, she shook her head. "I didn't hesitate. It's just a building. I've been back a few times for funerals, but I wasn't nostalgic. The Spirit isn't there anymore."

She paused. "I went to that building for decades and felt the Spirit, but now, I can just *feel* that the Holy Spirit is gone."

It wasn't initially so clear for Julia Mitchell. She'd been in the Episcopal Church her whole life. "There's no way," she remembers thinking. "I was not leaving the Episcopal Church." But then she thought about what her dad would have said—to follow her heart. She thought of the broader church's history. So many believers since the 1700s had left where they were to come to America. Puritans, French Huguenots. "Staying would be a break from tradition," Julia explained. "A tradition of putting Jesus Christ first, and seeking religious freedom to do so."

Others had concerns about what new structure the church would enter. Al Trakowski said, "I had my doubts about leaving. John had to reach to Africa to find a connection to the Anglican Church. I felt shaky about that. It was unstable." But still, he voted to leave.

Almost everyone did.

Yates remembers that the morning of the vote was very solemn. "We were not worried, not frightened." Others described the mood of the congregation as heavy and sober. Everyone knew it was a big day. The stakes were high—one member called it "the toughest decision I've ever dealt with." Some felt the significance of the vote was beyond the members' understanding. Some thought to themselves: *I hope we're doing the right thing.*

In his sermon that day, Yates spoke to these concerns. He told about how sad he was about leaving the denomination he had given his life to serving. But the Episcopal Church on the whole, he said, "bears little resemblance to the church the martyrs died to protect."

Yates took comfort in a note from a church member, which he had read the night before. The note stated, "John, I agree that it is extremely sad, especially for me, a lifelong Episcopalian. My grandfather said, 'If something is not right, it's dead wrong,' and the direction the Episcopal Church has taken is just that—dead wrong. I will be there tomorrow to worship and to vote for separation. I am praying for you daily and will help in any other way that you need help. As for the property, I pray that we keep it, but I'd still rather worship in a cornfield than submit to heresy."

The stakes were personal for Yates. They had implications for not only the church's future, but also for him. He recounted a conversation with his wife, Susan. He had told her about the vestry's strong decision to recommend separation.

"What does this mean for us?" she asked.

"It means that I can never retire!" he joked. Much work would lay ahead—hard work to advance down an uncertain road—and consistent leadership would be needed.

John explained to the congregation that joining the international Anglican family to establish a new North American church body would "demand great energy and a long time." This did not deter him. "Friends, I don't say it wearily. No, it energizes and excites me, because I believe God is doing a new thing in this century by joining the church in the Global South and the church in the East, with us here, in the West."

John laid out a vision of a church that would be international, biblical, sacramental, protestant, catholic in its unity, evangelical, and charismatic—all while maintaining an Anglican heritage and living sacrificially. "I believe that we are right now on the edge of a little wave that is slowly building energy and gaining strength, and it will one day become a revival—perhaps even a worldwide revival. God is doing something."

John paused, holding the congregation's attention. "I believe one day the historians will look back at this time and in a little footnote somewhere it will be noted that Anglicans in Northern Virginia took a step that proved critical in God's unfolding plan."

And so, with the humble proclamation of serving as a "little footnote" in God's plan, the church proceeded with its vote. The church's leaders were careful and thorough about the voting process, ensuring that there would be no pressure or potential for cheating. Church member and attorney Scott Ward had prepared a twenty-page memo that covered all the requirements for an effective procedure—under Episcopal rules and Virginia law. But the criteria for who could vote was simple: all active communicants in good standing.

The answer came back clear. Of the 1,348 eligible voters, 1,228 (90%) voted to sever ties with the Episcopal Church, and 1,279 members (94%) voted in favor of retaining the church's property. These results meant that even dozens of members who wanted to remain within the denomination believed that, if the congregation voted to leave, it should keep its property.

For some who voted to stay, the reason was the property itself. A few members did not want to risk leaving the beautiful historic property that George Washington had visited two centuries before, the place that had hosted their own special family occasions—weddings and baptisms and funerals—over the years. One man who had grown up in The Falls Church urged members not to leave. "We're not talking about Class A office space in Arlington, Virginia," he said. "We're talking about sacred ground."[54]

Others were not too concerned about the Episcopal Church's direction. Its leadership didn't necessarily affect this local church or its preaching or its beliefs. A few had gay family members or friends and felt loyalty to new, accommodating church doctrines. A combination of these reasons resulted in some members staying in the Episcopal Church. They began to meet in a Presbyterian church across the street. This was not easy. Divorce never is.

"It felt like being torn apart," Susan Yates said. The issues had become an immovable wedge between church members who had become like brothers and sisters. "It was very sad to see friends go," Jean Trakowski said. "It was like a family member saying he needed to move out of the house. We are still close."

The church still loved its Episcopal brothers and sisters. Even after the vote, the church always invited Episcopalians to the property and worship services. There was not enough space to host separate services for the Episcopalians on Sunday mornings, but the church shared facilities with former members for various events like funerals or weddings. While the local church thus showed love and accommodation in the midst of a painful division, tensions were only rising on the national and global levels.

Theologies Facing Off

The retribution of the Episcopal Church was swift and decisive. After a brief, court-ordered standstill, in early 2007 the Episcopal Church sued not only The Falls Church and others like it, but also their rectors and their vestry members. Battle awaited in the courts.

By February 2007, Bishop Lee—the man who had worked closely, in friendship, with John Yates for decades—had moved to eliminate Yates and others from the ranks of the Episcopal clergy. As a Washington Post article recounted about the "unexpected turn" of this "moderate bishop," he "removed the credentials of the conservative priests, declared their churches abandoned property and filed lawsuits asking courts to declare the churches property of the diocese, which comprises 182 congregations."[55]

Bishop Robert Duncan described this as a "sad, sad end" for Bishop Lee. They had worked together in the late 1970s. They were friends. "Bishop Lee's episcopate would have been recorded as one of the great ministries," Duncan said. "He was always in the middle, always tried to be fair to both sides, and in this one he winds up, as many see it, as the oppressor."

The tone of the debate grew more vicious. The press began to lambast The Falls Church and those like it who left the Episcopal Church. One headline read: "Episcopalians against equality." Another later referred to The Falls Church as part of an "Anti-gay Episcopal faction." The local paper went further, publishing an editorial the week after the vote—"Descent Into The Abyss"—claiming that "the church will go down in infamy as a regrettable and despised bastion of bigotry, prejudice and hatred."[56]

Much of the vitriol arose from how to frame the difference of the two sides: was this division about sexuality and tolerance, or about the Bible and the uniqueness of Jesus?

Yates and well-known church member Os Guinness responded with their own explanation in a Wall Street Journal Op-ed published in January 2007:

> We believe it is time to set the record straight as to why our church and so many others around the country have severed ties with the Episcopal Church. Fundamental to a liberal view of freedom is the right of a person or group to define themselves, to speak for themselves and to not be dehumanized by the definitions and distortions of others. This right we request even of those who differ from us.

Yates and Guinness explained that the core issue was theological: "the intellectual integrity of faith in the modern world." They also identified five ways in which the Episcopal Church had abandoned "the historic, orthodox Christian faith common to all believers." There was no mention of sexuality. "The *sola scriptura* ('by the scriptures alone') doctrine of the Reformation church has been abandoned for the *sola cultura* ('by the culture alone') way of the modern church." The op-ed noted "it is no accident that orthodox churches are growing and that almost all the great converts to the Christian faith in the past century, such as G.K. Chesterton and C.S. Lewis, have been attracted to full-blooded orthodoxy, not to revisionism."

These problems went straight to the heart of what it means to be a Christian:

> Episcopal revisionism obliterates the very identity of faith. When the great truths of the Bible and the creeds are abandoned and there is no limit to what can be believed in their place, then the point is reached when there is little identifiably Christian in Episcopal revisionism. Would that Episcopal leaders showed the same zeal for their faith that they do for their property. If the present decline continues, all that will remain of a once strong church will be empty buildings, kept going by the finances, though not the faith, of the fathers.
>
> These are the outrages we protest. These are the infidelities that drive us to separate. These are the real issues to be debated. We remain Anglicans but leave the Episcopal Church because the Episcopal Church first left the historic faith. Like our spiritual forebears in the Reformation, 'Here we stand. So help us God. We can do no other.'

The Yates-Guinness article stated that Episcopal leaders were denying the faith. That proved as clear with Bishop Schori as with any other leader.

Around the same time, a Time Magazine reporter interviewed Bishop Schori and asked, "Is belief in Jesus the only way to get to heaven?"

"We who practice the Christian tradition," Schori replied, "understand him as our vehicle to the divine. But for us to assume that God could not act in other ways is, I think, to put God in an awfully small box."[57]

This answer sparked immediate controversy. The very definition of Christianity revolves around Jesus Christ as the only savior.

Another reporter gave Schori an opportunity to clarify. This reporter, from National Public Radio, noted Bishop Schori's "interesting" answer to the Time reporter, and then asked, "What are you: a Unitarian?!"

Bishop Schori and the reporter laughed together. But the reporter pressed the question. "What are you—that is another concern for people, because, they say Scripture says that Jesus says he was The Light and The Way and the only way to God the Father."

Schori was no longer laughing. "Christians understand that Jesus is the route to God," she said. "That is not to say that Muslims, or Sikhs, or Jains, come to God in a radically different way. They come to God through . . . human experience . . . through human experience of the divine. Christians talk about that in terms of Jesus."

The reporter again sought clarification. "So you're saying there are other ways to God."

Schori did not deny it. "Human communities have always searched for relationship with that which is beyond them . . . with the ultimate . . . with the divine. For Christians, we say that our route to God is through Jesus. That doesn't mean that a Hindu doesn't experience God except through Jesus." She hesitated. "It says that Hindus and people of other faith traditions approach God through their own cultural contexts; they relate to God, they experience God in human relationships, as well as ones that transcend human relationships; and Christians would say those are our experiences of Jesus; of God through the experience of Jesus."

The reporter tried to process this answer. "It sounds like you're saying it's a parallel reality, but in another culture and language."

"I think that's accurate," Schori said.[58]

This was not about homosexuality. This was about Jesus Christ—who He is, whether what He says in the Scriptures is true, and what that means for humanity. But on every issue, Schori parted from the beliefs of most Christians.

On the issue of reproduction, Schori was asked, *How many members of the Episcopal Church are there in this country?* She answered, "About 2.2 million. It used to be larger percentagewise, but Episcopalians tend to be better-educated and tend to reproduce at lower rates than some other denominations. Roman Catholics and Mormons both have theological reasons for producing lots of children." *Episcopalians aren't interested in replenishing their ranks by having children?* "No. It's probably the opposite. We encourage people to pay attention to the stewardship of the earth and not use more than their portion."[59]

On the topic of abortion, Schori stated, "We say it is a moral tragedy but that it should not be the government's role to deny its availability." She also supported the U.S. government's mandate on all employers, regardless of their beliefs, to provide birth control.

These statements led many within the church to question her theology. The more people questioned her, and the more she explained, the clearer her views became. In her opening address before the entire Episcopal General Convention in 2009, she said, "the great Western heresy—is that we can be saved as individuals, that any of us alone can be in right relationship with God."

Yet Jesus told the criminal hanging beside him on the cross, "today you will be with me in Paradise" (Luke 23:43). He also said, "Whoever hears my word and believes him who sent me has eternal life. He does not come into judgment, but has passed from death to life" (John 5:24).

Schori's views could not be reconciled with Christ's words, nor could they go without a response. Yates took to the pulpit at The Falls Church to make sure the positions were clear. He brought to bear his reflections on the key theological changes sweeping through the Episcopal Church. Remembering this sermon, a church member said, "It was one of the most powerful sermons I've ever heard."

Discernment and Holy Communion
John Yates, Sermon on November 5, 2006

I have observed an alarming development. It's a devaluing, even a profaning of the Lords' supper through a gradual development of a very different understanding of Christ's death. Now in the words of Jesus himself, in the words of the apostles, in the words of the church fathers, in the words of the reformers, indeed, throughout the history of the orthodox church, there's been one central, essential principle that has bound us all together and that is that Jesus died for all people and it is only through the doorway that he opened to God on the cross that anyone can come to know God's saving grace, God's loving embrace. This is the message of every book of the New Testament. This is the gospel. . . .

We have a new presiding bishop—you can read all about her in today's Washington Post and Washington Times. [*Yates recounted her interviews above with Time Magazine and others.*]

Now friends, this sounds really good. It sounds thoughtful; it sounds open, humane, kind, unassuming. Any pathway to God works, one works as well as another. The trouble is, friends, this is not Christianity. This is universalism. It's not Christianity. And in spite of all the beautiful and orthodox language in our Book of Common Prayer, more and more of those who read it aloud in worship no longer really believe it. . . .

Now according to this new way of thinking, the apostles were wrong, the church fathers were wrong, the reformers were wrong. They were all guilty of putting God in an awfully small box and Jesus himself must have just been wrong about this or else he's really misquoted in the Bible because of the scores of times he refers to himself as the unique way to God.

These are the two issues on which this whole current denominational controversy is based: the authority of scripture—is the Bible true—and secondly, the unique exclusivity of Jesus Christ. All the hubbub about sexual sin—it's not unimportant. But these are the two cancers that are consuming the life and the health of our denomination.

Now . . . I believe to receive Holy Communion when I have not really submitted to the unique claim of the gospel is to spit in God's face. If I don't need a savior, then why did God send his son to the cross? He's up there on that cross looking down and saying, *If I didn't have to do this, why am I up here?*

Would you, if you were God, would you do that to your child if there was another way? If this is true, all the saints and martyrs died for the faith and the gospel in vain, needlessly.

I want to be as clear as I possibly can. Jesus did not say, "I am a way to God, but you know, if you're from Rome, you might be happier worshiping Diana in the temple down the street. More power to you." He didn't say that. His claim is to exclusivity.

We cling to a unique savior, and an exclusive gospel in a pluralistic world. We cling to an authoritative Bible in a skeptical age. We cling to a sacrificial lifestyle in a consumer culture. We cling to a pure and chaste life in an era of permissiveness. We say the creeds without crossing our fingers. We trust in the reality of heaven. We trust in the reality of hell. We proclaim Jesus as the only hope of salvation. The work of God in Christ and the word of God in scripture are complete. We can add nothing else. We believe that the local church can be the hope of the world. We are plain, simple, mere Christians. That's what we are.

Now, I just want to ask you, are you willing to face 21st century persecution? It can be painful. But what really frightens me is that we might *not* face 21st century persecution! If we aren't meeting rejection, if we're not being dismissed, it shows we aren't being bold and we aren't sharing the gospel of Christ. We aren't engaging the culture; we're remaining silent because we don't want to offend anybody. Where is courage? Where is conviction?

It's right here, I hope. Are we going to be like the Corinthians? Are we going to profane God's holy gift, downsizing Jesus to be hardly any better than Muhammad or Buddha? Are we going to boldly submit to Jesus as the Lord, the way, the truth, the life? That's the gift we celebrate in the sacrament.

My dear friends, you have to decide this for yourselves. I can't decide it for you. In a moment or two, we're going to stand and say the creed. As we stand, don't be pressured to say it if you don't believe. But if you do believe it, or if you're struggling with it but you want to believe it, say it with all your heart, because in it is the truth, the way, the life. Amen.

* * *

After John Yates's sermon that morning, the congregation stood. They said the words of the creed with meaning, with faith—their voices filling the building that the congregation had built, and that would soon make them prove how far they would go for their words.

12

To The Courts

In the first place, when you come together as a church,
I hear that there are divisions among you. And I believe it in part,
for there must be divisions among you in order that
those who are approved among you may be recognized.
1 Corinthians 11:18-19

Litigation can always be avoided, in theory. Property has a value, and the disputing parties can negotiate about what that value is. Church property is no different—even a multi-million-dollar, historic property like the land and the buildings of The Falls Church. The departing congregation could have kept the property, and the Episcopal Church could have received compensation for it. Businesses do this every day. But the Episcopal leadership was not willing to discuss value. The dispute had reached a deeper level.

Presiding Bishop Schori directed that American dioceses must not sell parish properties to breakaway groups. She said the church expected a "reasonable and fair" deal on any property settlement, but that "we do not make settlements that encourage religious bodies who seek to replace The Episcopal Church." She even recognized that her policy would allow the buildings to be used as saloons, but not by fellow Anglicans.[60] In testimony under oath, Bishop Schori later confirmed that she refused to allow congregations to purchase the buildings they had been using, regardless of the amount of money they wanted to pay, if they were going to affiliate with another province of the Anglican Communion.

In 2011, Bishop Schori's position led to an extreme result. A New York church that had left the Episcopal Church had offered to pay for the building in which it worshiped. This was not an option. As one article put it, "the Episcopal Church sued to seize the building, then sold it for a fraction of the price to someone who *turned it into a mosque. . . .*"[61] Another source noted that "the Muslims used a crane to remove the cross. A sign on the building now reads, 'Islamic Awareness Center.'"[62]

As a consequence of this hard line drawn by the Episcopal Church, many congregations that voted to leave the Episcopal denomination simply walked away from their buildings. Other Episcopalians opted to disaffiliate entirely from Anglicanism to reduce the risk of losing their buildings and spending years in expensive litigation. Schori had admitted that if a congregation left the Anglican Communion—such as becoming Baptist or Methodist—negotiation would at least be possible. Only those who left the Episcopal Church but wanted to remain Anglican would be guaranteed a fight in the courts.

The ultimate result of Schori's policies was painful litigation in nineteen states. The Episcopal Church dedicated well over $20 million to legal actions against departing clergy, congregations, and dioceses. Several churches leaving the Episcopal Church in South Carolina and Texas eventually prevailed and kept their property. Churches in seventeen other states did not.

But nowhere was the litigation more complicated and costly than in Virginia.

Early Victories

The Civil War ripped apart many churches along Northern and Southern lines. In 1867, following these divisions, the Virginia government passed a law to determine which congregations would keep their property. The law survives intact to this day, and it is found in Section 57-9(A). The main part reads:

> If a division has heretofore occurred or shall hereafter occur in a church or religious society, to which any such congregation whose property is held by trustees is attached, the members of such congregation over 18 years of age may, by a vote of a majority of the whole number, determine to which branch of the church or society such congregation shall thereafter belong.

After such a church "division" and vote, the majority of the congregation could go to court to be "approved" as the trustee with title and control over the property. The process might sound simple, but it requires a judge to decide thorny religious issues. First and foremost, had a true "division" occurred?

Between December 2006 and January 2007, eight congregations, including The Falls Church, filed petitions under this Virginia statute. The churches declared their "division" from the Episcopal Church and sought court approval to keep their property. The Episcopal Church sued these congregations in return, plus three others, seeking court orders that the congregations be restrained from using and occupying the properties. A storm of other claims and counterclaims followed.

The attorneys working on behalf of The Falls Church faced a serious mandate. David Gustafson, vestry member and judge of the U.S. Tax Court, charged the attorneys: "You represent The Falls Church, and The Falls Church represents God; do nothing to dishonor God in this litigation." The lawyers heeded those words, carefully crafting their arguments and submitting reams of legal briefs and evidence. They also coordinated efforts among eight different law firms representing the eleven different churches involved—each with their own property and history. These included other prominent congregations in the area, such as Truro Church, Church of the Apostles, and St. Stephen's Church.

The eleven separate church cases were consolidated into one case in the Circuit Court of Fairfax County, under Judge Randy Bellows.

The stage was set for a trial in November 2007. The key question was whether the old Virginia statute, Section 57-9(A), could be invoked in the litigation. If so, the statute would likely allow The Falls Church and others like it to keep their property. Winning would require historical expertise about the meaning of the 19th century law.

In fall 2007, mere weeks before the trial, the churches faced an important deadline: submitting their list of experts. They had one expert, Mark Valeri, but there was a sense that someone else would be needed. The day before the deadline, one of the church's lead lawyers, Steffen Johnson, was driving to his child's soccer practice when he received a call. It was John Yates.

"I know a guy who went to college with my son," John said. "He might help. Why don't you give him a call?"

Steffen arrived at the soccer field. He called the potential expert, Charles Irons. Steffen began to explain the issues, but he didn't need to say much. He listened in shock as Dr. Irons discussed in detail Section 57-9(A) and its history after the Civil War. Dr. Irons knew this off the top of his head. He had a Ph.D. in American History from the University of Virginia, and his focus was Civil War divisions within Christianity. The next day, Dr. Irons' name was on the list of experts submitted to the court.

Dr. Irons went on to research the historical record in detail. Pouring through the paper archives in Virginia, he located twenty-nine petitions similar to the ones that The Falls Church and those like it had filed. They became powerful support for the case.

Days before the trial, tensions were high. The stakes were clear. Yates wrote to the church encouraging them to pray for Judge Bellows. "I am praying that he will decide this case in our favor, but sometimes what we think is best may run counter to God's larger plan. So I pray that in ruling justly and wisely he will be immune from any outside pressures that might cause him to reach a result that is not pleasing to God."

The trial spanned five days in November 2007. Judge Bellows

conducted the proceedings fairly. The experts had an opportunity to testify. Gordon Coffee and Steffen Johnson of the law firm Winston & Strawn played a leading role. Things seemed to go well. Many left the trial hopeful that the separating churches would prevail.

After months of waiting, victory came in April 2008. In a detailed 80-page decision, Judge Bellows ruled in favor of The Falls Church and the others like it. The decision recounted the ways in which church leaders found themselves "taking sides against their brethren" and resolving to "walk apart," causing "a level of distress among many church members so profound and wrenching as to lead them to cast votes in an attempt to disaffiliate from a church which has been their home and heritage throughout their lives, and often back for generations."

On the issue of whether a "division" had occurred within the meaning of the Virginia statute, the judge concluded that "it blinks at reality to characterize the ongoing division within the Diocese, [the Episcopal Church], and the Anglican Communion as anything but division of the first magnitude." The judge noted how important the experts were for his decision. He found the departing churches' experts "to be more persuasive and convincing." In particular, he singled out Dr. Irons as "especially helpful to the Court in understanding the early history of 57-9." A timely phone call on a soccer field had helped secure the win.

But both sides knew it was the first battle in a longer war. Appeal was coming. Yates asked for prayers that the church would be able to contain its legal expenses. "Our reserve on the general budget oscillates between 17-30 days of operating expenses. This is a thin margin." The church gave generously, and the litigation wore on.

Even after another favorable decision by Judge Bellows in December 2008, there was no great celebration or showmanship. Yates wrote to the church about the news, calling for more prayer. He encouraged people "to stop and give thanks and praise to the Lord for these results." He recognized that the lawsuit would continue to appeal, with more demands and stress. "But God has graciously helped us keep focused on our mission, and we have sensed profoundly His blessing at every stage of this journey. We have so much to be thankful for as we enter this Christmas season."

The Virginia Supreme Court

By the spring of 2009, the Episcopal Church had appealed to the Supreme Court of Virginia. Church leaders perhaps sensed the tenuousness of the moment. At the end of an update about Easter services, Yates beseeched the church "to bring this extremely serious matter before God in your own prayers. I cannot imagine how we could be better represented from a legal standpoint. Still, our dependence is upon God. We pray He will be most glorified in the outcome, and that the outcome will be most favorable for the health of His church and spread of His gospel."

Life in the church went on. Those who were not directly involved in the litigation could almost proceed as if it did not exist. Lawyers worked behind the scenes, crafting their briefs for the appeal. The church remained in possession of its property—which continued to burst at the seams—pending the litigation.

A year later, in 2010, the parties presented their arguments before the Virginia Supreme Court. Those who attended the hearing recalled that the courtroom was a sober setting. The justices, as might be expected, focused narrowly on several fine points of the law—mostly regarding the Virginia statute from the 1800s.

Steffen Johnson argued powerfully on behalf of the church. Scott Ward and Hugo Blankingship—the attorney who had argued in the Righter trial years before—joined him at the table. The Attorney General and the Solicitor General of Virginia had also become involved, presenting arguments in favor of The Falls Church.

And yet, Yates recalled leaving the hearing without confidence about the outcome. His confidence in God, however, was unshaken.

He wrote to the church: "It may be that our prayers matter more now than previously, because the justices are now going to be deeply engaged in considering this case and formulating their own conclusions. . . . We are truly in God's hands. He has so wonderfully overseen and provided for us over the years, and I have absolutely no doubt that He will continue to do so." A couple months later, and a couple days before the decision, Yates wrote again: "I know you will join me in praying continuously that the good and perfect will of the Father will be done in this matter."

Many church members prayed. God always hears the prayers of His people, but His answers are not always what His people expect.

The decision came down in June 2010. It was a complete reversal. The Falls Church had lost.

The Virginia Supreme Court held that the Virginia statute, Section 57-9(A), did not apply to the dispute between the Episcopal Church and the departing congregations. Perhaps rubbing salt in the wound, a key basis for this decision was a finding that, "while undoubtedly there was theological disagreement," there had been no "division in the Anglican Communion" such that the statute would apply.[63] Without the Virginia statute supporting its claim to the property, The Falls Church and those like it had only standard property and contract law arguments left to make—they faced an uphill legal battle. The case was sent back to the lower court to decide these issues.

At this point, the case looked grim. It could have been a time to mourn. But Yates encouraged the opposite. Here's what he wrote to the church:

I will bless the Lord at all times. His praise shall continually be in my mouth. Psalm 34:1. . . . We can be confident that the ruling is not the 'final judgment' in a spiritual sense. And all this week I have been reminding myself of what we do know for certain in this matter. We know that:

God is real. God is good. God is all knowing and all powerful.

God has called us to a walk of faith and obedience through Jesus Christ.

Jesus promised his followers not only a full and abundant life, but trouble, affliction, and pain. We walk the way of the cross, which is the way of life everlasting, but a life of hardship as well.

Any lack that we may have is an opportunity for us to learn afresh that God loves to bless us, supply our needs, and guide our steps.

Nothing can separate us from Him.

And nothing did, even as the litigation continued. When Yates took his annual prayer retreat in the summer, he asked the congregation to "skip a meal or two specifically for the purpose of using that time for prayer." The tone had shifted. The focus of the prayer was not the property or winning the litigation. The first item was "that this lawsuit might soon end and be resolved in a way that somehow is a witness to the greatness of God to our community, and that all of us involved might live fully into whatever God plans for good to come from this lawsuit. That somehow the reputation of Christ be enhanced through these things."

The next trial came in spring 2011, again before Judge Bellows. While the first trial had lasted one week, this trial was six long weeks spanning April, May, and June. One attorney described the first trial as the "air war," and this one was like "the house-to-house fighting in Baghdad." The sides presented their cases, with detailed arguments about history and old deeds. The trial took 22 days and put over 60 witnesses on the stand. The witnesses included John Yates and other church leaders.

"It was painful," Yates said. "It was just too personal. It felt like going through a divorce—an amputation of thirty years of my work for renewal—and then being judged for that divorce. I felt under attack."

The time for preparation and other legal matters also took Yates away from his ministry. He could not devote as much attention to it as he wanted and had in the past.

The legal issues were far from simple. The facts were contested. Their implications were argued. After the trial, the parties each submitted briefs tallying hundreds of pages. Falls Church members Scott Ward and Steffen Johnson played leading roles for the legal team. They and others at their firms had prominent litigation practices and devoted thousands of hours to this case—at steeply discounted rates. The church could not have asked for better representation. But they also met worthy legal adversaries, led by David Beers and Bradfute Davenport on behalf of the Episcopal Church. With advocacy at such a high level, the parties aired all their arguments. They left no stone unturned.

The ultimate question, as framed by the court, was whether The Falls Church property was held in trust by the congregation, in light of the deeds being in the name of The Falls Church and the property and buildings paid for by its members. The deeds of other CANA congregations were also at issue in the case, posing many of the same issues. The Falls Church had one unique argument: it had existed even before the creation of the Episcopal Church that it was now leaving.

While the congregation waited eagerly for the court's decision, the summer brought a sign of what lay ahead. On July 3, 2011, the church gathered for "one big, happy celebration" at Bishop O'Connell High School. Yates announced the news with a prophetic line: "O'Connell has a large auditorium big enough for our congregation to gather together." He explained the service and the plans for a huge picnic. "I think this will be one of our happiest and most memorable experiences EVER."

It was a great picnic. A few years later, the church would enjoy many more memorable experiences at this large Catholic high school.

The second half of 2011 passed without a decision. One evening Yates invited the church to "Vision Night." He shared "about the year ahead and what things I believe God has in store for us as a church.

This is a pivotal year." A few months later, in the lead-up to Christmas, and still in the losing stages of a legal battle, Yates wrote about the "signs of God's great blessing and favor upon us as a church. . . . Even though this is not an easy season for many and as a church we face large challenges, the crowded worship services, the healthy sense of anticipation in the face of our uncertain future, the quality of men and women willing to stand in next month's vestry election, these things are so encouraging!"

Soon after the turn of the year, this optimistic message gave way to more disappointment. On January 10, 2012, Judge Bellows—the same judge who had ruled in favor of The Falls Church a few years before—issued the decision that paved the path for final defeat. The judge's reasoning gave "dispositive significance to the fact that, while the CANA Congregation is still *called* 'The Falls Church,' it is no longer an *Episcopal* entity."

The decision ordered The Falls Church and all its sister churches to give their properties to the Episcopal Church. This property included Washington's church—the same one built in the 1700s when the old one was "rotten and unfit for repair." The property also included, to the grave disappointment of many, all monetary donations given by church members prior to January 31, 2007. That date was well after the church had voted to leave the Episcopal Church, and after the members had clearly designated such funds specifically for The Falls Church.

The church, reeling from the loss, considered whether to continue seeking justice through the legal system. Yates asked himself, the vestry, and the church: "Is God calling us to continue in litigation for perhaps one to two more years, or is He leading us to something very different now?" Many meetings and more prayers led to the decision to stay with the case, to see it through.

One reason, as Yates wrote on May 24, 2012, was the example of "Paul's determination to appeal his false arrest in Jerusalem and trial at Caesarea to the Emperor in Rome. He judged that to use the legal system of his time was appropriate and in no way compromised his faith. Paul's purpose was simply to be a faithful steward of all that the Lord had entrusted to him, above all the Gospel of Jesus Christ and the power of the Holy Spirit to transform lives."

Another reason for continuing to pursue the litigation was that the church had the resources to do it, while many smaller congregations did not. A legal precedent in favor of The Falls Church could aid those smaller churches.

So the case pressed onward.

Yet The Falls Church enjoyed no more victory. The court ordered the church to transfer the property and depart from the premises by May 13, 2012. The church lost its partial rehearing before Judge Bellows.

Then, on April 18, 2013, the church lost its appeal to the Virginia Supreme Court. The court came up with a theory—which none of the parties had argued—for why the Episcopal Church would keep the property. Without analyzing the relevant deeds, the court imposed a "constructive trust" on the property. It found that The Falls Church had violated a "fiduciary duty" arising from a 1979 denominational trust known as the Dennis Canon—passed by the Episcopal Church the same year that John Yates had come to The Falls Church. This Episcopal trust was prohibited by state law when it was passed, but the court ruled that the Dennis Canon and "the course of dealing between the parties" showed that The Falls Church had agreed and expected that its property would be held in trust, with itself as trustee, for the benefit of the Episcopal Church.[64]

In a twist of fate, the decades of steadfast work for renewal within the Episcopal Church by Yates and others—rather than outright fighting against the denomination—had now been turned against them. The Virginia Supreme Court found that this "course of dealing" only confirmed what the Dennis Canon had attempted to do in 1979, that is, to force The Falls Church into the role of a trustee for a denomination that it was now leaving. Thus, the great irony of the court's reasoning was that the loyalty of The Falls Church and its leaders to the Episcopal Church over many years only contributed to defeat in the courts.

Litigation is hard. Losing litigation is even harder. The congregation weathered over six years of litigation, with costs dwarfing the annual budgets of many churches. After presenting the church's case, carefully and persuasively, with the full backing of earnest prayers, the outcome was loss, loss, and loss. The congregation lost its building, its land, and over two million dollars in cash.

But they gained what matters most.

As Judy Thomsen, who had served as Yates's assistant in the 1980s, put it, "We were doing this for the sake of the Bible . . . . Maybe that's why the sermons got even better after we lost the property."

13

Loss for the Sake of Christ

But whatever gain I had, I counted as loss for the sake of Christ.
Philippians 3:7

For whoever would save his life will lose it, but whoever loses his life for my sake will save it. For what does it profit a man if he gains the whole world and loses or forfeits himself?
Luke 9:24-25

You can tell a lot about people by how they respond to adversity. This is as true for groups as it is for individuals. Consider the Jewish people of Moses' time when they left Egypt. They lost their homes. They trekked through a desert, they were hungry, and they grumbled. They made a golden calf and worshiped it instead of God. God punished that generation by making them wander for forty years, so that only two of those who had left Egypt made it into the Promised Land. Even Moses got only a glimpse of it.

Consider also the apostles. When they lost their leader, Jesus Christ, they were confused. They went into hiding. It was not until Jesus returned, and until they received the Holy Spirit, that they were ready to spread the word.

Now consider the congregation at The Falls Church. Would they grumble and face God's punishment like the Israelites? Or would they go into hiding like those early apostles before the Spirit came?

The church did something entirely different.

It worshiped.

Hope in Defeat

Allison Gaskins, the daughter of John and Susan Yates, remembers the text message. She sat in the crowd of a middle school band concert. Her mom Susan delivered the news: "We lost everything."

Coldness washed over Allison. For a moment she was stunned, in disbelief. As the words sank in, she knew she had to go home to be with her parents. Their family home—which the Episcopal Church could take any day—was quiet and somber. The lights were off. It felt as if someone had died.

Allison remembers her dad spending a lot of time on the phone with the attorneys that night. They had to understand the decision and its implications. They had to prepare to break the news to the church. They had to plan next steps. Allison knew her parents well, and she had a powerful sense about her father's role. "He was one, small, tired man, holding this up."

A few days later, John Yates wrote a message to the church. "It is understandable that this ruling is upsetting to many. You may be having feelings of anger, grief, fear, or just uncertainty. This is surely normal, and healthy. While we are strongly affirming our trust in God, at the same time it isn't good to ignore or deny feelings like this. God gives us the gift of emotion and we are wise to talk and pray with others about our feelings. Better to deal with these emotions now, honestly, than to sweep them under a rug and then have to confront them later."

Yates went on to explain that grief and other hard emotions should be put in context. The church's faith called for hope.

> I believe that hopefulness is the word for us just now. St. Paul said that we 'do not grieve as others do who have no hope.' (1 Thessalonians 4:13) What does this mean? Let me share with you what a retired bishop wrote to me recently. He said, 'You remind me of Vaclav Havel's distinction between

optimism and hope: Hope is definitely not optimism. It is not the conviction that something will turn out well, but the certainty that something makes sense, regardless of how it turns out.'

Hopefulness simply means we trust that our Lord God will bring us through all of this, and that one day, as Jesus promised the disciples, we will understand and it will be well. This hope may not keep us from some grieving but it supersedes, it is stronger than grief or anger. The greatest of all outcomes would be if all of us, every one of us, were somehow transformed through this experience, changed into Christ-likeness. For to be like Him is the greatest of all possible outcomes."

Yates's rhetoric contrasted sharply with the local press's portrayal of his position after the loss in the court. One article described him as "the leader of the breakaway congregation . . . officially defrocked." It presented his choices as either "to leave and take as many breakaway congregants as he can to another location, or to step aside and permit a reconciliation of the two groups."[65] As usual, outsiders attributed more significance to Yates's role than he would to himself. But one thing was clear: this "breakaway congregation" would be staying together.

On January 15, days after the loss, Yates was in the pulpit—a place where he has always shined. On stage, this "tired man" looked younger, stronger, and six inches taller. His words, in the midst of difficulty, soared.

When Jesus Was Put Out of the Church
John Yates, Sermon on January 15, 2012

Yates began with a description of a church gathering on the heels of their loss the prior week: We had an amazing evening together, close to a thousand people here . . . . It was an evening of great thanksgiving and praise in spite of bad news. It was actually one of the most amazing gatherings in my life.

It was very different from two years ago, when we had been before the Virginia Supreme Court. . . . I remember when we came together that night, several hundred of us to pray, I just felt so heavy. I felt so discouraged that it took me several weeks to work through that to figure out what God might be saying. But as we came in here Thursday night, I did not have any sense of that heaviness or darkness or burden. It was just sheer joy to be here with God's people together.

There's much about this that is extremely sad for us, but I've never had a greater sense of God's blessing upon us and God's desire to lead us forward. I don't know how our gathering the other night could have been any happier if we had won the case rather than lost it. So, I appreciate that strong feeling again this morning.

Yates then preached about the meaning of God's justice—how it was not limited by human views of justice, and how "To live in justice is to live like Jesus." His message captured the spirit of the church in that moment, a spirit that seemed impossible after the staggering loss just days before in court.

It is ironic that my assignment—preaching on justice—came the week when we were told that the law court of Virginia told us that we must leave our home here behind, and that all we have here belongs to the denomination that we left behind years ago. To me, it's a strange thing that our courts would decide that all of our property belongs to a denomination simply because they announced that they owned it thirty years ago, though they didn't pay for any of it, they invested nothing in it. To us, it doesn't seem just. This seems so clear to us that we could hardly take in the ruling. It was like a punch in the gut. Should we continue to fight it? Should we continue to spend money trying to keep what we believe is ours?

A mother told me this morning of a dream her child had last night or the night before that has got me really thinking. I've been worried about the children in the church. How are they going to handle all this? And she said, 'Let me tell you a dream my daughter had.' She said it was a dream about us. And she said we were swimming in a pool, and it had sharks in it, and we climbed up onto a wall for safety. And on the other side of the wall was a big sea, where we were called to go. And we had to be pushed off the wall into the sea where we could swim safely.

And you know, I'm just wondering, maybe we're being pushed off the wall now. Maybe there's a whole new sea for us to be swimming in. We don't quite know yet.

This is a hard decision we face. We asked God's guidance. Certainly this judge would not have ruled against us, all seven of our churches, if he had not been convinced that our reasoning is wrong. And many judges around the country in similar cases have agreed that our reasoning is wrong when they've voted for other church situations. Still, appeals may be possible; they may be warranted. But just now it's not clear to us. It's just not clear right now, although you can imagine that in a church like this, many people have many ideas about strategies for us to pursue, and they're bringing them forward! Boy, we've got some smart people in this church!

But we have some time. We do have thorough plans for relocation, which are, in fact, pretty exciting. They'll be difficult, but pretty exciting. The judge has ordered that we must pay our old denomination a huge amount of money in addition to turning over the property to them. This is, in some ways, the hardest part of this decision. I'll have to tell you more about that later this morning.

Forced relocation may very well be God's way of pushing us out, just like the early church was forced out of their home in Jerusalem. It just may be that the time has finally come for us to follow the model of the early church . . . .

When Jesus was put out of the church, what did he do? He withdrew, he reconsidered his mission. He carried on, doing what he was sent to do, and doing it in the spirit in which he was sent to do it, not loudly complaining, not quarrelling.

We are not going to complain in this church. We will not speak harshly of the Episcopal Church. We will not speak of winning or losing. We will prayerfully, like Jesus, consider our options. We will study the word of God, and God surely has more to show us than we've seen thus far. We'll be listening. And we'll do this with you, the larger church . . . .

Living through this lawsuit has helped us realize a couple of things. One thing that's been clear to me is we have learned a whole lot more about the need for each of us to be growing up into maturity in Christ. And the other thing we've learned is that we can plant daughter churches, and we've planted six or eight of them. And they're doing pretty well.

There are other things we have to learn. We have much more to learn about how we're to live together as a church according to this larger definition of God's justice. God desires a just world, and it has to begin in this church. If non-Christians can look at a church like ours and see us actually living out God's blueprint for mankind, if people can see that we're healthy and fulfilled and generous and compassionate in expressing and experiencing the power of the Holy Spirit and caring sacrificially for our neighbors, if people see that, then anyone who has a heart for God will be drawn to that. And if we're honest and kind, if we're people of integrity, of compassion working on behalf of the poor, people who have a heart for God will be drawn to that. And if marriages are being healed, and if broken relationships are being reconciled, and if addictions are being broken, and if we're reaching out and helping one another in the hurting places, people who have a heart for God will be drawn to that, wherever we're meeting. If the Holy Spirit is working among us in power, and in forgiveness, and making people whole, and if we're living holy lives, if we're making sacrifices for the sake of people less fortunate than we are, people who have a heart for God will be drawn to that. And when we're honestly working through our various vocations and in the community to bring healing where sin has wrought such destruction, anyone who has a heart for God will be drawn to that.

And friends, you know the reason the world is in such a mess, the reason we have so much misery, poverty, addictions, enmity, slums, pollution, people abusing and using each other just to achieve their own pleasures, the reason for that is that people are chasing false gods. People are asserting their own will rather than seeking the will of Christ. And if that's true of you and me in any way, now's the time to see it in our own lives and confess it and repent of it and get on further into the justice, the kingship of Christ.

Life is just too short to chase after things like comfort and security or having your own way—I mean, there's nothing wrong with those things. But our goal has to be to become the people of God in every way possible, and not settle for anything less, and to call others to join us. And perhaps all of this upset that we're experiencing now, perhaps somehow this will push us further into that.

I remembered this morning the end of the Narnia tales, where Aslan calls all of his children, and he says, "Come further up! Come further in!" And I felt like he was saying to us, "Come further in! Come further up into what I've created you for!"

Now there's a vision! There is an exciting vision. If losing this dear church will help us enter into that, then it will have been worth it. And if this is true, then we're right on the verge of some radically new experience. And many more people will be touched through our little church than we've experienced so far.

This is a good place for us to be in. It's hard, but it's good. And together we'll find our way.

14

Sending Away The Best

Churches with healthy DNA must be reproducing themselves. I'm so pleased that The Falls Church is seeking to do this. The Timothy Program has the potential to provide wise mature young leaders in our nation's capital and beyond.
Tim Keller, Founding Pastor,
Redeemer Presbyterian Church, New York City

The Falls Church was gaining in its loss. In fact, its membership *increased* as it prepared to leave its historic property. During that time it was not unusual to have nearly 3,000 people present on Sundays, between worship services and evening youth gatherings. Perhaps it was the continued force of the preaching, or the powerful example of a group of people taking a stand—whatever the cause, newcomers streamed through the doors.

Churches can handle rapid growth two main ways. They can continue to amass numbers and horde their talent, or they can start sending people away. For many years, the Episcopal Church had resisted the efforts of The Falls Church to plant new churches nearby. That was not a good business model, particularly for a denomination with steeply declining numbers. But after The Falls Church had left the denomination, it became free to send out its new young leaders. Something powerful was about to begin.

* * *

David Glade had been through the Falls Church Fellows Program. He had gone to seminary and been ordained. Now he wanted to start a new church.

It would be one thing if a new pastor wanted to train and learn at The Falls Church, and then move to an existing church that he would lead. Starting a new church was a much riskier proposition. The costs were high. A new church did not have established members or a budget, much less a building.

But young pastors like David Glade had a vision, and The Falls Church helped to hone that vision and bring it into life through the Timothy Program (the name inspired by 1 Timothy 4:12). Under this program, the church would help teach and train the young pastors. The church would also pay the pastor's salary and benefits for the first three years at the new church.

That was not cheap, but the greater cost came in human form. Not only would The Falls Church be losing this young leader it had invested in, but it also encouraged its own members leave, if they felt led by God to do so, to support the new church plant. The new churches formed in the same area—a few of them within ten miles of the "mother" church. Several daughter churches took around one hundred members each. These weren't members on the fringes. Every time a new church started, it would take with it some of the most committed members of The Falls Church.

This is profoundly counter-cultural, even within the religious community. "Most pastors have a business like anyone else," one member explained. "They are supposed to grow their churches. They're supposed to build up contributions. What John Yates did was counter to all that. Between the Fellows, the Timothys, and the church plants, John sent away the best. John always had that vision."

In addition to those risks and costs, The Falls Church invested much in the pastors who came through the Timothy Program. The church selected them, paid them, trained them, and connected them with established mentors. Yates would meet with them regularly. He would advise them on their sermons. He would take them out to his farm in the countryside, just to get to know them better.

In 2009, as part of a celebration of the Yates's 30 years at the church, many of these men had an opportunity to explain what they had gained.

Bill Haley founded St. Brendan's in the City in downtown Washington, D.C., after working in the church and leading the young adults ministry for years. He had this to say: "I can think of no better person to have been mentored by and supported by as a church-planter than John Yates, and mostly I'm grateful to God for the privilege of being able to be under such tutelage."

"I remember the day John called me," said David Hanke, who became the pastor of Restoration Anglican of Arlington—just a few miles from The Falls Church. "I was outside the chapel at Gordon-Conwell and I quickly abraded a long path in the thread-bare carpet as I paced back and forth. He invited me to be a part of this new 'Young Timothy' program and to think about planting a church inside the beltway. I jotted down notes from our conversation on a hymnal because I couldn't find paper. That was a phone call that changed my life. In John's leadership, I have seen many things I admire: his unusual perseverance and long-suffering to lead one church for a long time; his prayerfulness; his choice to listen to many voices before making a decision; his trust in people and delight in the gifts they bring; his devotion to excellence and hard work."

Patrick Ware founded Winchester Anglican 70 miles west of The Falls Church. He spoke about learning the lesson of patience. "Waiting seems to be part of anything of real substance that John does. Waiting, studying, praying, and asking for an abundance of counsel. I've grown to very much appreciate this—it will be invaluable to my leadership in the coming years! What a gift to give a pastor for life; the desire to wait upon the Lord and to trust his timing and his people."

Another distinct feature drew Sam Ferguson to work under John

Yates. John's son had mentored Sam in Philadelphia, and he recommended that Sam meet his dad. So, at a conference in Jerusalem, Sam did just that. He had no idea John led such a large church. He showed up for their coffee wearing a t-shirt and flip flops. John, not one to judge based on attire, saw promise in Sam and invited him to intern at The Falls Church during Sam's time in seminary.

Sam came for the summer, and as he learned about the church, what he learned made him want to come back. "Excellence," Sam said. "Obviously The Falls Church stands apart for many good things. But it was the excellence of it that drew me."

Sam explained that one of his concerns about ministry was that some men chose it rather than the business world because it was less work. That's not what Sam wanted. He sought diligence, and he found it in Yates. The congregation had many hard workers, and Yates could relate to them because he worked hard, too. "Each sermon took hours of refinement," Sam said. "It took professionalism. That's what I'm learning here."

David Glade, the former Fellow who came back as a Timothy, founded Christ the King Anglican Church in neighboring Alexandria. He'd spent much time with Yates over the years. He explained that he'd been "taught" much, but what was even more profound were the lessons he "caught" just by spending time with his mentor:

> I caught a vision for prayer. A quick walk through John's office reveals hundreds of pictures tacked to a wall board. I've sat in studies and noted the same thing as he leafs through his Bible—pictures, tucked amid the chapters. As he opens his journal, sometimes a picture will escape, fall to the floor, only to be picked up and placed back between the pages; pictures of parishioners and co-workers, pictures of his wife and family, maybe a picture of you, maybe a picture of me. Why all these pictures? These pictures help John pray for the people in his life, to look at those countless pictures, recall each name and bring each name and the concerns they carry to the Father in

prayer. I take great comfort in the fact that John prays for me, and John has given me a vision of a pastor who prays.

I caught a vision for personal Bible study. A reading from *Encounter with God*, a psalm and a chapter from the gospels, these are the ingredients that make up John's morning diet of Bible study, a diet I have followed per his encouragement. It may sound obvious. 'Of course,' we may think, 'pastors study the scriptures.' But so often the events of the day and even the preparation of a sermon can drive out personal time in front of God's Word. For John, behind every sermon he delivers, every session of counsel and word of advice there stands a tremendous reservoir of personal Bible study. John has given me a vision of a pastor who studies God's Word.

I have caught a vision for the hard work of pastoral ministry. In my time at The Falls Church there were very few mornings that I arrived earlier than John, few evenings I stayed later. John approached his work with intentionality, diligence and thoroughness. He has taken ideas like the Fellows Program, like the Timothys Program, and through partnership with others and his own hard work those ideas have become a reality.

I have caught a vision for the local church. Perhaps my favorite reflection about John and The Falls Church is that despite the size of the Falls Church—and it is massive—despite the impact of The Falls Church—and it has a tremendous impact—despite the renown of The Falls Church—and The Falls Church is known around the nation and even other countries—despite all these accurate and well deserved accolades, The Falls Church has always struck me as simply a local church, striving to be faithful and led by a humble pastor. John has given me a vision for the power and impact that lies within the local church.

Like David Glade, pastors have continued to plant new churches after the Timothy Program. In 2011, Johnny Kurcina founded Christ

Church Vienna in his hometown eight miles away from The Falls Church. In 2012, Wright Wall founded All Nations DC in Washington. Dan Marotta will soon be founding Redeemer Anglican Church in Richmond, Virginia. These many young pastors have taken pieces of The Falls Church experience with them as they start their own churches. Many of these newly planted churches thrived, acquiring their own buildings and growing quickly.

One instrumental person in helping these young pastors succeed was Bill Deiss. Bill was the parish administrator who oversaw many aspects of church life. Bill had come to the church in the mid-eighties and became a close friend of John Yates through Bible study and work together. Bill's background as a trained scientist with international business experience, combined with his love for Christ and tremendous sense of humor, made him a key person in the life of the church. The young Timothies came to see Bill as something of a dad and still go to him for advice regularly. He now serves as the Executive Director for the Anglican Relief and Development Fund.

The Timothy Program and its church plants demonstrated how The Falls Church was growing through adversity. In 2012, Bishop John Guernsey used The Falls Church as an example of how crisis and persecution "can stir the Church to obedience to the Great Commission and to bring many to salvation":

> I am so very thankful for the witness and leadership of The Falls Church in Northern Virginia.
>
> When the crisis hit The Episcopal Church in 2003, The Falls Church responded by planting a church among the poor in Washington, D.C. When The Falls Church left The Episcopal Church in 2006 and was sued, they responded by . . . planting another church. Millions of dollars were drained away in litigation before they received a first round victory in court. Their response . . . was to plant two more churches. Then the positive ruling was reversed on appeal and they were sent back for another trial. They responded by planting another church.

This time they lost at trial and they were forced out of their buildings this spring. Their response—you guessed it—has been to prepare to plant another church this summer.

After sending out clergy and parishioners to plant six churches, The Falls Church has grown by over a third in nine years, and the combined average Sunday attendance of The Falls Church and these six church plants is more than double what The Falls Church's was in 2003.

This was not irony. It was God's design of pruning and growth. The church that had lost its property and was sending out its best continued to thrive. The people had become a family that stuck together and attracted others. With the Lord's guidance, Yates would begin to lead them away from their place of comfort and security and through the wilderness of Northern Virginia.

15

Moving Out

Anyone who puts his hand to the plow and then looks back
is useless for the Kingdom of God.
Luke 9:62

In the spring of 2012, The Falls Church prepared to move out of
the property that, centuries earlier, George Washington had graced.
The church would walk away from the colonial building and its history,
the cemetery with the remains of family members, and the well-worn
office halls. It would leave the soaring sanctuary that its congregation
had built, that had hosted hundreds of weddings and baptisms. It
would even leave the prayer books, the sound equipment, and $2.8
million in cash that members had donated to church accounts
designated specifically not to go to the Episcopal Church.

Everything worldly about the church had to change. The worship
space. The offices. The website. Even the church's name. There was
no longer "The Falls Church." Now there was the "The Falls Church
Episcopal" in the historic place, and The Falls Church Anglican
without a place to call its own.

On March 2 and 3, the church gathered together to worship. The
church had long been giving praise to God, and these difficult
circumstances were no exception. "In the midst of this time of
upheaval and uncertainty in our congregation," Yates wrote, "we are
being reminded afresh to place our hope and trust in the goodness of

God and to set our minds on Jesus Christ. There are few better ways to do this than to gather together and lift our voices in worship." Worship leader Jamie Brown led a packed house to make a live worship album over those days. The album—*A Thousand Amens*— captured "the cry of a congregation that has learned and clung to the reality that Jesus is worthy of costly worship."[66]

While the church worshipped, it continued to face criticism for its decision, mainly by the press. The church held to its convictions, but did so with grace. In a public statement, Yates kept his focus on the Kingdom. "The core issue for us is not physical property, but theological and moral truth and the intellectual integrity of faith in the modern world. Wherever we worship, we remain Anglicans because we cannot compromise our historic faith. Like our spiritual forebears in the Reformation, 'Here we stand. So help us God. We can do no other.'"

Yates encouraged members to follow his lead with their words. As the church was still grieving, preparing to leave, he addressed a common question: what should members say about the misinformation in the community? "You know, when I read some of what is in the press about our church, I think to myself, I wouldn't want to be involved in a church like that." He offered some advice. "When you get into conversations about this, do not be defensive and do not be resentful. As the Proverb says, 'Malice backfires. Spite boomerangs.' Smile, speak in love. God will do the rest."

A few weeks before the move, Yates gave a vision of what lay ahead. It was not a prosperity doctrine. Such a message would have rung hollow for the long-time members of The Falls Church. Far from worldly riches, Yates kept the focus on eternal things. Just days before leaving the place he had long called home, where he had devoted his passion and his work for over three decades, he delivered a message from deep within his soul about God's promise.

All Things Work Together For Good
John Yates, Sermon on May 6, 2012

We are in a sensitive moment now, this church family of ours. About to move out of our familiar surroundings, not of our own choosing, not—to our way of thinking—a fair or just decision. We have been stripped down, in a sense, to the basics.

Required by law, we have had to give up most of our financial resources, prevented now from using those funds for the purposes for which they were given. In a very few days now we will say goodbye to this lovely, light-filled sanctuary which we built twenty years ago, say goodbye to the classrooms, the books, the Bibles, our beloved and holy little prayer chapel, the old church, the grounds we have loved and tended for so long, the library, the bookstore, the kitchen. Clergy and choir robes will be left hanging in their place, these chairs will be soon empty, offices where so many confidential and prayerful discussions have taken place, will be empty. . . .

Many details for our path forward remain unclear, and we know the adventure ahead is going to be challenging. But, we move forward with an invigorated feeling of purpose.

In a sense, this will be like starting all over again, with no resource except ourselves and our God. There is a teaching in the New Testament: when you are at your weakest you actually are at your strongest. In weakness we are forced to trust in and depend on God.

St. Paul said that God told him, "My grace is sufficient for you, for my power is made perfect in weakness."

We know that where God leads us is a good place. There is much about all this that I do not understand, but I take comfort in the words of Christ: "What I am doing now you do not understand. But afterwards you will understand."(John 13:7)

The greatest of all outcomes for us at The Falls Church would be if all, every one of us, were transformed through this experience, changed into Christ likeness. For to be like Him is the greatest of all possible outcomes. . . .

Our sovereign God, responding to the Holy Spirit's cry on our behalf as we seek to follow Christ, turns everything around for the best end.

Now look, don't misunderstand! If some brother loses his job, you cannot tell him that he will get a better one, because God is working all things for the good. Or you can't say to a friend not to be upset because his fiancé broke up their engagement because this must mean God has an even better partner waiting for him somewhere.

If someone fails to be accepted at the college she always wanted to attend, you can't, on the basis of this, promise her that she will get into a better school. No, the mistake that people make with this promise in Romans 8:28 is they understand the "good" that is promised from too narrow and materialistic a perspective. Yes, God is working in all things for the good, but that doesn't necessarily mean that, having lost this lovely sanctuary, God will give us some place that is even better, larger, more beautiful. I certainly hope he does, but this is not what the verse means.

The "good" that God promises is His good for us, so that we, His children, will grow up to be like Christ. . . .

The promise here is not that every difficult experience will always lead to something else good in this life—it may, it may not. God may remove us from secure, well-paying jobs to simply shake us until we realize that we have been living a lifestyle that is, frankly, extremely materialistic and not honoring to God and the priorities He has for us.

He may be removing us from these wonderful facilities because comfort and convenience have become a substitute for genuine commitment.

One week later, John Yates implored the church to have courage:

I don't want to tell you what your emotions should be. But I do want to suggest what your thoughts should be. Your thoughts should be this: God is for us. . . . We're about to enter into a great and wonderful time of inconvenience. There's going to be setting up, tearing down. We'll be meeting in unfamiliar places. They won't be as beautiful as this. . . . It's going to be messy.

Some of you will find this annoying, confusing, upsetting, and a little thought is going to cross your mind: *maybe I'll just stay home this Sunday*, or *maybe I'll find another church*. You will have these kinds of thoughts. . . . Will our commitment be so strong that we laugh at inconvenience and push on through it?

Yates then told a story about George Washington and Thomas Paine and the continental army in the 1770s. Many soldiers were "sunshine patriots" who fought only when the weather was good. Paine wrote pamphlets with the famous words: "These are the times that try men's souls." Yates continued:

I don't want to be a sunshine Christian. I don't think you want to be either. Now you have an opportunity to show that you're more than that. Will you commit yourself to no complaining? No grumbling? But rather to reject those thoughts and to take it in stride? Hard times will come—society is changing so radically—and this time can help make us stronger.

Joshua 1:9 says, "Have I not shown you, be strong and of good courage. Do not be frightened, and do not be dismayed, because the Lord your God is with you wherever you go." God is for us. Dangerous times may come when it requires great courage. If you are faithful to Him now with these little challenges, you will be prepared to be faithful if bigger challenges come.

The Last Day at the Historic Property

John Yates had done his best to speak the truth of God's promise for the church, to share an uplifting but honest spirit. His teaching could dampen the blow of loss. But it could not take away the loss. The loss had to be suffered before it could produce gain.

And so the last Sunday at the property came on May 13, 2012.

Virginia Watson, a church member in her nineties, recorded her thoughts in a letter about the last service at the historic church. "I worshiped at my last regular Sunday morning Eucharist in the Historic Church. The church was full, the day bright and beautiful, the music inspiring. . . . Mostly it was an inspiring worship service not too different from an ordinary Sunday."

She explained, however, that several things were unusual. "There were two inserts in the service leaflet; one was a pledge card asking for an increase in giving. I filled out my card and left it with the usher. The Falls Church was required to deposit on hold with the courts a check for $2,800,000, everything we had in our accounts when the suit was filed. This leaves us pretty broke."

Most people at the church felt that way at the time. The loss of those funds was like salt poured in the wound of losing the building.

Virginia then described the other insert in the leaflet. It was "a bright yellow card that John asked us to date and, if we were so moved, to write a recommitment of ourselves to God. I did. I thanked God that nothing can ever separate me from His love and that it is my desire to be His faithful follower all the days of my life. I dated it, signed it and put it in my Prayer Book."

The church had lost its tangible assets, but it doubled down on its faith. This was important for the changes ahead. As Virginia described it, "the leaflet had the new mailing address for the church, a PO Box, a new phone number, and a map with directions to the school where we will meet on the next two Sundays. There was also an announcement that we would exit the church while singing the final hymn and go out for lemonade on the lawn. Since I sit on the front row I led the exit on my side of the church. It seemed like a long aisle, and many thoughts raced through my mind. I was sad but my primary emotion was to stand tall and straight, to be courageous, to trust God, and not look back. . . . Of course I remember the service we had when [my husband] Frank died and the church was full of those who wanted to give thanks for his life. I shall miss sitting on the first row that has kneelers where Frank sat beside me."

It was a special day. So special that Virginia also attended the service in the main sanctuary and the evening service. In the main sanctuary, Virginia wrote, "every seat was taken and some people had to go to overflow closed circuit TV coverage. The service was mostly praise music, drums, lively, loud, clapping—energetic, and joyful." But the joy was not light-hearted. One reporter who attended the service noted "that grown men cried during the last song, 'In Christ Alone,' as everyone lifted their arms in the air."[67]

At the evening service, ten young men spoke. Nine of them were from the Timothy Program—the pastors who had either planted new churches or were about to do so. The tenth was Gary Haugen, whose International Justice Mission had been established from a men's Bible study in the church. The ten men's words captured the powerful impact of the church, both in their lives and beyond. Yates also gave a short talk. He explained that, "soon after he arrived at The Falls Church, over thirty years ago, he was very aware that God's word had been faithfully preached from this pulpit by many before him." Then Yates prayed that "God's word would continue to be preached and that those who worshiped next in this space would be blessed."

Yates's prayer—the defeated asking blessings for the victors—touched Virginia Watson. "It was such a humble and godly way to respond. What we want is for God to be glorified. . . . I will miss the sweet soft reverence and silence. There is something about a prayed-in place that enhances worship. For 280 years this had been a house of prayer and a prayed-in place. It is hard to end the chapter and turn the page."

Virginia closed her written memories of that last day with a handwritten note to John. It read, "You have done a magnificent job as our leader in this wilderness time."

Nearly 4,000 people attended those services on the last day. As John described it: "In the last two weeks we left well and began well! Our final Sunday on the property was as sweet and joyful and faithful as anything we have ever experienced."

The church's leaders prayed over the property and prepared for the new rector and staff. Unknown to John, his daughter Allison baked a cake with the message "Welcome"—and left it as a gift for the incoming Episcopalians. Another team patched the walls and cleaned up. A last picture taken of John at the property showed him vacuuming a tiny room where he had worked on his sermons for decades.

Everything was in good order for the next occupants.

Then the people of The Falls Church left. God's grace and peace had escorted the church away. A locksmith changed the locks behind them.

The following Sunday, the Episcopal denomination returned to the property. One reporter who visited that day found "a quiet, empty campus. One little girl sat on a swing on the playground after church, a playground that was full of children the Sunday before. The main sanctuary, where the Anglican congregation filled the pews and overflowed onto the floors feeling the blast of the organ, was empty and silent, the lights off."[68]

The Final Chapter of the Dispute

While the church had left its property, some chance, however slim, remained that the Supreme Court of the United States could overturn the Virginia decisions. This prevented a sense of finality from settling.

It was a hard question whether to appeal to the U.S. Supreme Court. It would be costly, and the church had already seemed to move on. Yet most of the vestry wanted to take this step. The church, unlike many others, had the resources—however strained—to pursue this. The church's attorneys still believed their case was strong. Yates and a few others were opposed, but in a spirit of compromise, they ultimately unified around the decision to appeal.

In the end, the church lost again when the Supreme Court chose not to take the case on March 10, 2014. It was not surprising, given the long odds of the Court taking any case, but unlike the prior court decisions, this one brought complete finality. There was no avenue left open for appeal. The church had pursued this course to its end.

Yates gave voice to this closing chapter of the church's history. He explained the church's belief that pursuing this legal process was part of its ministry. He gave thanks for the justice system that allowed the case to be heard, and he offered prayers for "the many churches and dioceses that remain embroiled in lawsuits over their property with The Episcopal Church or other denominations."

But above all, Yates reminded the church of God's perspective. "The legal process may be finished, but in the end only God's judgment is final and only God's judgment matters. Our prayer has always been that God would be pleased with us for fighting the good fight, finishing the race, and keeping the faith."

16

An Anglican Movement

Do not be conformed to this world, but be transformed by the renewal of your mind,
that by testing you may discern what is the will of God,
what is good and acceptable and perfect.
Romans 12:2

No one felt this conflict quite like Nicholas Lubelfeld.

Nicholas, like many within The Falls Church, had long and deep ties to the Episcopal Church. He was also an Episcopal priest. He received his seminary degree from Virginia Theological Seminary, and served an Episcopal church in Lansing, Michigan. Then he became the rector of another Episcopal church in Northern Virginia. He led that church for seven years, but the match never quite worked.

As Nicholas left that position and sought other positions, he came to attend The Falls Church as a worshiper. "I wanted to do school ministry," he said. "I told John Yates, I could work here, but put me at the bottom of your supply list."

Maybe Yates sensed Nicholas's gifts. He is a fiery, committed man—his faith like unmovable ballast that pins down his curious energy and his occasionally spirited tongue. "I'm the rumpled fellow in a church with a preppy patina," Nicholas said.

Yates hired Nicholas first as a pastoral associate on a part-time basis. Then it was full-time—for over twenty years. His focus has always been pastoral care. Or, as Nicholas summarized it, "I've baptized babies who are the fruit of unions I've solemnized."

Like most at The Falls Church, Nicholas is evangelical. Ever since he was ordained, he felt like a minority within the Episcopal Church. "My spiritual temperature was hotter than my classmates in seminary."

Nicholas believes the Bible is the authoritative Word of God. He was disappointed by the results of the Righter trial and the ordination of Gene Robinson. And Nicholas would never be shy to express his views boldly.

But in December 2006, when nearly all members at The Falls Church voted to leave the Episcopal Church, Nicholas didn't participate. "Had I voted, it would have been against leaving," he said. "I kept my oath. I can remain in the Episcopal Church as long as the Bishop does not command what God forbids."

Nicholas recalled a talk that John Stott, a renowned Anglican theologian, gave at The Falls Church in 2006. "Stott said that even if there is material heresy in the church, he could still teach in the church. But when that heresy becomes a formulary—written into the church's catechism and constitution—he couldn't stay in it. I agree with that. People have been tolerating bad teaching as long as I've been in the church. The laws are still fine. Policemen are misbehaving."

Of course, as with the litigation, things were not simple for those caught up in these issues. Nicholas stayed with The Falls Church as it left the Episcopal Church, even if he didn't vote and didn't necessarily support leaving. Yates agreed to that and told Nicholas, "No one is going to lose a job for staying."

Nicholas was surprised, however, when he saw his name among those priests "inhibited"—placed on warning that they might be deposed from their ordination.

"I wrote to Bishop Lee," Nicholas said. "I explained that I remained in the Episcopal Church. I had never done anything against it, but I wanted to continue pastoring at The Falls Church."

Bishop Lee agreed to remove Nicholas from the "inhibited" list. Yates and Bishop Lee met and worked out an arrangement in which Nicholas would serve another Episcopal Church in the area on a part-time basis, while he remained with The Falls Church. This agreement between Yates and Lee, despite their many conflicts over recent years, showed the possibility of grace and healing.

But as the conflict wore on and deepened, it no longer remained possible for Nicholas to stay at The Falls Church without joining the new Anglican denomination—the Anglican Church of North America (ACNA). Nicholas had been classmates with Bishop Martyn Minns of ACNA. "I asked Martyn if I could be ordained. Martyn said he would license me, even with my Episcopal ordination. 'All I care about is whether you're sound or not,' Martyn told me."

Nicholas faced more challenges on the Episcopal front. "I met with Bishop Lee after joining ACNA." Nicholas smiled, but his pale gray-blue eyes seemed sad. "I told him I was going to stay."

"That's a pity," Bishop Lee said to Nicholas. "We may have to depose you."

"I know," Nicholas replied.

"I'm so sorry."

"Will you give me your blessing?"

"Of course," Bishop Lee said, and he blessed Nicholas.

For a man of such exuberance and energy, it is clear that this conversation, this moment, left a deep mark on Nicholas. "It's like divorce." The word "divorce" slipped out of his tightly pressed lips, showing his pain at the very notion of it.

Afterwards, Nicholas said, "things were a lot less rancorous." This was not necessarily a good thing, in his mind. He would rather have the rancor and the unity than the peace and the separation. "I was talking with a close friend of mine who stayed in the Episcopal Church. He told me, 'Frankly, it's such a relief that you're gone. We can get on with missions now.'"

Both sides seem to feel that way. There's a sense that it could have been an amicable divorce, if not for the property and the prohibitive edicts from Bishop Schori and other national Episcopal leaders. The divorce instead had to go to court. Whether amicable or not, however,

Nicholas's place in the conflict should serve as an important reminder: divorces always bring pain.

The Episcopal Church is forever changed, because it lost many important congregations and endangered its role in the Anglican Communion. The Falls Church is also forever changed, because it lost its building and its denominational heritage. Yet God moves through these changes. Sometimes a person, or a church, has to give up much to gain even more.

The Anglican Church of North America

The Falls Church did not float in a hierarchical vacuum after it left The Episcopal Church. For a few years, it operated under the Church of Nigeria, through a missionary body called the Convocation of Anglicans in North America (CANA). This led the local press—the same paper that had labeled the church a "bastion of bigotry and prejudice"—to now label the members as "rightfully called 'the Nigerians.'"[69]

While a more permanent structure awaited, disputes waged in the Anglican Communion. Church leaders from the global South continued to press for change within the Communion to address the changing doctrine and practices of the Episcopal Church. They also spoke out against the litigation proceedings. In August 2007, Archbishop Peter Akinola of Nigeria wrote to his fellow Anglican Primate, Bishop Schori, in response to her request that Akinola not install Rev. Martyn Minns as a bishop of CANA:

> You mention the call to reconciliation. As you well know this is a call that I wholeheartedly embrace and indeed was a major theme of our time in Tanzania. You will also remember that one of the key elements of our discussion and the resulting Communique was the importance of resolving our current differences without resorting to civil law suits. You agreed to this. Yet it is my understanding that you are still continuing

your own punitive legal actions against a number of CANA clergy and congregations. I fail to see how this is consistent with your own claim to be working toward reconciliation.

Property litigation had placed a wedge between the two sides that none of their attempts at reconciliation could overcome. Tensions remained high as the Anglican leaders approached another significant meeting. The Lambeth Conference of 1998 had been a lightning rod for contentious issues of faith, especially sexuality. Ten years later, it was time for the next Lambeth Conference.

In 2008, however, a month before the gathering of the Anglican Primates, a smaller portion of bishops and leaders—many from the global South—met for a conference in Jerusalem, the Global Anglican Future Conference (GAFCON). After seven days of discussion, the GAFCON participants issued their conclusions. They stated that their movement arose because of the "false gospel" of the Episcopal Church and others that had departed from Biblical views on sexuality and the uniqueness of Jesus Christ. GAFCON declared its traditional tenets of faith and prepared to continue as a movement, rather than as a one-time event.

When the full cast of Anglican leaders met a month later at the Lambeth Conference in the United Kingdom, the Archbishop of Canterbury did not reopen the controversial resolution about marriage from the prior Lambeth Conference. He instead explained that the "listening process" continued on issues of sexuality. Several archbishops who had attended GAFCON declined to attend Lambeth, effectively boycotting because of the practices of the Episcopal Church, and furthering the divide within the Anglican Communion.

Orthodox Anglican leaders in North America had been supported by the global South—many of the GAFCON participants—over years of turmoil with the Episcopal Church. The time had come, however, for them to take their own step forward.

On June 22, 2009, these leaders met at St. Vincent's Cathedral in Bedford, Texas. Evangelicals such as Rick Warren spoke to the audience, commending their stance. Representatives from the global South also attended. Years of prayer and planning came together as the leaders created the Anglican Church in North America (ACNA).

ACNA, like the broader Anglican Communion, provides for a wide range of church practices—from those nearly Catholic in their worship to more evangelical and contemporary. ACNA allows for ordination of women as priests, but not as bishops. It holds the traditional view of marriage and does not bless same-sex unions. Unsurprisingly, the ACNA constitution and canons make clear that each local church, not the denomination, owns its property. Many hard lessons had been learned from the litigation against the Episcopal Church—and the drafter of the ACNA constitution, former Falls Church Chancellor Hugo Blankingship, made sure those lessons were put to good use.

At the time of its creation in 2009, ACNA had just over 700 congregations and almost 70,000 in average Sunday attendance. Four years later, in 2013, it had over 900 congregations and well over 100,000 in average Sunday attendance. Many Anglican provinces, especially in the global South, immediately embraced ACNA. But, to this date, ACNA has not received official recognition from the Archbishop of Canterbury or the full Anglican Communion. Its position within Anglicanism, while growing and taking clearer form, remains unsettled.

Robert Duncan was the first Archbishop of ACNA. His successor, Foley Beach, took office in 2014. At his investiture ceremony, a former Anglican archbishop read a message from Pope Francis, sending his "personal greetings and congratulations as he leads his church in the very important job of revival."

The Falls Church within ACNA

Archbishop Beach visited The Falls Church Anglican in May 2015. He made clear how important the church was to the global movement. He expressed thanks for the church's witness, both within America and throughout the world. But he also had personal thanks to convey.

John Yates interviewed Archbishop Beach briefly before he preached in the high school auditorium in Northern Virginia. He asked the archbishop about his family and his path. Beach said he'd been married to his wife for 32 years, and that they'd just celebrated their anniversary the prior week. The congregation applauded for them.

"That's a good start," Yates said.

"We're still taking lessons from you," the archbishop replied. He went on to explain how Yates "has been a hero of mine." He said that when he and wife had young children, Susan's book on parenting was a huge help.

At the end of the service, the archbishop looked to Yates before saying the benediction. Yates urged him on. That little exchange and others showed that even the highest ACNA leader respected Yates and his role in the Anglican Communion. It showed that leadership does not require titles and vestments. Leadership is earned and practiced, and Yates had done that through years of stormy weather. As church member Cherie Harder described it: "our congregation has been schooled by a Rector and vestry that have met confusion with prayer, opposition with courage, attacks with humility, setbacks with grace, and uncertainty with faith."

Perhaps John had drawn lessons from a founder of Anglicanism, Thomas Cranmer, about sacrificial leadership. He told this founder's story in a sermon in 2006—days before the church had voted to leave the Episcopal denomination.

The Reformers (on Thomas Cranmer)
John Yates, Sermon on November 26, 2006

After discussing Anglican heritage, and how it is "shot through with grace," John told the story of Thomas Cranmer, the first Archbishop of Canterbury and the author of the Book of Common Prayer in the 16th century.

I don't think anyone has ever had a greater genius about prayer, praise and worship and about people coming together to worship God. Thomas Cranmer was certain that the Bible needed to be in the hands of all people. He convinced King Henry VIII to have the Bible translated and published. He saw that it was disseminated.

But, as a young man, he never had any idea of going into the ministry. He wasn't religious. He grew up on a farm in the country, the son of a minor squire. He loved the girls.

When he went off to Cambridge to study, his professors found that he had a brilliant mind. He set academic records. But he threw away a promising academic career because he loved the daughter of the tavern owner in his home town and he went back and married her.

Tragically, within a few years, she and their infant child died. This almost killed Tom Cranmer. It nearly finished him. He was not by nature heroic, and if it hadn't been for the friends from his University days who came to him, I doubt if we would have ever heard from him again. His friends gathered around him in support. They comforted him, encouraged and prayed with him, stayed with him and got him through. Eventually, he returned to academics and pursued his career.

He became a clergyman and one of the best-known, revered Christian scholars in Britain. He was twenty-eight years old when Martin Luther nailed his 95 Theses to the door, and he began to study everything he could get hold of, he and his scholarly friends at Cambridge and Oxford. These future church leaders would gather at a little tavern, the White Horse Tavern, and they would study the Bible and drink beer together every week. They were known affectionately as 'little Germany' because they loved the writings of the German reformer Luther. These men had become convinced of the reliability and the reasonableness of Luther and the other continental reformers' teachings.

Legend has it that when a plague swept through, Cranmer, in his late thirties, fled to an inn in the country, near London. Unexpectedly, King Henry VIII retreated to the same place. They had never met each other, but at this country inn the king and the clergyman became instantaneously close friends. It was a friendship that led to a new church in Britain.

Three years later, Cranmer became Archbishop of Canterbury. The church broke from Rome, and Cranmer annulled the loveless marriage of Henry to Catherine, who had been the widow of his older brother.

The story of those days is complicated and not all pretty. There were days of political intrigue, terrible pressures upon Cranmer. Cranmer, along with the other reformers who were appointed to leadership in the church (men like Latimer, Ridley), built a new, reformed church in England. Then, Henry VIII died and his little son Edward VI was made king. Edward was a godly, pious child and during the years of his reign he was discipled by Cranmer and together set the church in England on strong Protestant footing.

The boy king died as a teenager and his older sister Mary, the daughter of the spurned queen, Catherine of Aragon, an ardent Roman Catholic, ascended the throne. Cranmer's days became numbered at that point. Now in his mid-sixties, he was imprisoned at the Tower of London for months and months. Eventually he and others were transferred to prison in Oxford. The stories of the martyrdom of their friends around England filtered through to them.

Barely subsisting in prison for over two years, Cranmer's health broke. The solitary confinement was desperately hard on the man. The queen and her newly appointed church leaders periodically dragged him out, subjected him to repeated inquisitions, and threatened him with his life. Often, his conditions were harsh. Food was meager at best. Sometimes he was not even allowed his manuscripts, writing materials, or Scriptures. He was repeatedly ill. His two best friends in the world, his brothers in the faith and partners in the reformation, Latimer and Ridley, were both burned to death at a stake right outside the window of his prison and he was forced to stand at the window and watch their suffering and death.

Cranmer began to waver. His courage ebbed and flowed as he was challenged and ground down psychologically. Visitor upon visitor urged him to avoid death and return to Roman Catholicism. In Rome, an effigy of Cranmer was hoisted and burned. Finally, after years of extreme stress, his steadfastness broke. Lonely, exhausted, worn down, bewildered, this old man signed a document repenting of his Protestant views. In fact, he signed several documents over a period of weeks. He betrayed the Reformation he had led.

Quickly, the Queen's representatives and church authorities spread the word. They organized a public gathering in which Cranmer would announce his change of thinking. They had told him they would free him and he could live. But then, they changed their mind and he learned that whatever he said or did, his days were numbered.

The night before he was supposed to speak publicly renouncing his reformed faith, he made up his mind to do something courageous. Exhausted, he saw that he'd rather die than go back on the Biblical truths which he had dedicated his life to. And so, on that rainy March morning, standing in the pulpit of great St. Mary's church, before all the authorities, all the representatives of the queen and the church, Cranmer shouted out his allegiance to the faith for which his brothers had already died. Totally unexpected, pandemonium broke out. The people there were enraged. They had planned to kill him anyway. They got quickly about their business.

As one historical text describes it: "Chaos ensued. The Archbishop was pulled from the platform, dragged through the streets of Oxford to the very spot where Latimer and Ridley had suffered six months before. The spectators quickly caught up with the execution party. There was little time for farewells. Cranmer was stripped to his shirt and chained to the stake. Earlier, in the commotion at St. Mary's, he had promised that his right hand would be the first to burn 'for writing contrary to my heart.' Now, as the fire began to take hold, Cranmer stretched out his hand into the flames for all to see, crying out loudly, 'This unworthy right hand, this hand has offended.' And although it was a wet morning, the fire burned freely, fiercely, and the Archbishop died quickly with the words of Stephen on his lips: 'Lord Jesus, receive my spirit. I see heaven opened and Jesus standing at the right hand of God.'"

So many of the stories of the martyrs throughout history have been stories of great unflinching courage and bravery. Cranmer's story wasn't like that.

John's sermon concluded with a message directly for the church:

Our patron saint, Thomas, was one who wavered and broke, just like you and I have time and time again. I think that's why I love him so. And yet, he regained his faith and courage, and you and I have, too.

We love the church for which he died. We wish it could be perfect. We know from time to time it needs to be awakened and reformed. We believe such a time is here again.

17

Tabernacle

And he said to them, "Take nothing for your journey, no staff, nor bag, nor bread, nor money; and do not have two tunics. And whatever house you enter, stay there, and from there depart. And wherever they do not receive you, when you leave that town shake off the dust from your feet as a testimony against them." And they departed and went through the villages, preaching the gospel and healing everywhere.
Luke 9:3-6

Living without a home is hard. There is no regular place to lay one's head. No assurance of warmth or a dry bed. But Jesus did not call believers into an easy life. He instructed his closest friends to "take nothing" as they journeyed, preaching the gospel.

It's easy to imagine how the disciples drew attention in this state. They'd wander from village to village with nothing but a tunic. They'd tell the people about Jesus, and their voices surely had a note of desperately zealous energy. They had nothing but words and hungry bodies. As darkness fell, they'd seek a place to stay. Those who opened their homes were blessed. Those who rejected them were cursed.

More than ever before, The Falls Church Anglican could resonate with these disciples. Where does a church of several thousand people meet when it doesn't have a home? A congregation needs a gathering place. It was possible, of course, for the church to splinter into smaller churches. Many members could have gone to the daughter churches that had been planted in the area.

But by now it should be clear: this people had become a family. They were going to hold together. They just had to figure out how.

A Church Without A Home

Jesus repeatedly warned that the Christian life was not comfortable in worldly terms. When He said that it was more difficult for a camel to pass through the eye of a needle than for a rich man to enter heaven, he made clear the dangers to the soul of a person without needs. It was the poor and the destitute who most craved God.

The Falls Church Anglican was neither poor nor destitute, but for the first time in many years, it felt real, great, and pressing needs. The church had to lean on others, and that brought many blessings. An early sign of such blessings came from an antiques dealer out of Pennsylvania. He had heard about the church's litigation, and its losses. He wanted to help. And so, with no advance notice, he arrived to donate a full array of communion silver that he had been collecting for decades.

Churches in the area—Catholic, Baptist, Presbyterian, and many others—also rose to meet the congregation's needs. The Catholic Church, through Bishop O'Connell High School, provided a new, temporary church home. The auditorium had blue, plush chairs, a solid stage, and a crucifix hanging above it. Classrooms became Sunday school and nursery spaces. The school library hosted classes on baptism. The courtyard hosted picnics and lemonade.

But even this large high school could not meet all of the church's needs. Smaller gatherings of various ministries met at other locations. Some services were held at the chapel of Rivendell, a local Christian elementary school. Services were also held regularly at Columbia Baptist Church. This large, classic brick church—with its white steeple piercing the skyline within view of The Falls Church's old historic property—hosted many services. The more formal 8 am service met there almost every week. Francis Long and her husband, mentioned before as one of the few members who had been at The Falls Church even before John Yates, were so thankful to Columbia Baptist Church that they gave the church their grand piano as a token of gratitude.

When Bishop O'Connell was not available, because of school plays or graduation or other events, the church held its Sunday services in local public schools. These included Kenmore Middle School, George Mason High School, and the Falls Church High School. Other times none of those were options. The church met on a few occasions in the banquet rooms of the Fairview Park Marriott or an auditorium of the NOVA Community College.

None of these options were free. Several were very expensive.

This constant shuffling also required immense logistical and moving support. A moving church is no easy thing. It's a little like a rockstar's tour that keeps going for years. Every week the church had to move a grand piano, a digital organ, a drum set, and other musical equipment. This didn't even count the tables, the toys for childcare, and the communion silver. The groupies of a rockstar tour fade out over time, but the church needed scores of volunteers every week to prepare for worship.

In spring 2015, Yates took a few moments from a Sunday service to interview someone who helped with the setup every week. "We're at a halfway point," Yates said. "There are still lessons God wants us to learn in this period. It's time for a second wind."

The man who came to the stage—in a public high school auditorium—had started coming to the church in January 2014. This was well after the church had left its historic property. "I'd been coming a few months," the man said, "and John said we needed more people to help for about three straight weeks. So I figured there was a need."

The man explained the work that he does. Carrying instruments and chairs. Checking the sound system. "Plugging the wire into the organ is the best part," he said with a laugh. "It makes this great click, and then, when the organ starts playing, I have the immediate gratification of knowing that I helped make that happen. I served our church that way."

As well as Yates led, and as strong as the church family was, moving every week from location to location—with all the setup and logistics required—took its toll. Some difficulties were trifling. "Let's be prepared again to 'laugh at a little inconvenience,'" Yates suggested.

The church did that with minor issues, like when it met at a local public school but a major parking area was not available. "Sneaker Sunday," the bulletin announced. Yates told the church it was the first-ever "1K walk." He invited everyone to park in the church's offices—temporary offices—at a nearby office complex. Someone would be there to give people a trail map, and they could walk on a nice path through the woods—"there's trees, a creek, some ducks"—to get to the high school. "It's going to be a great adventure," Yates said, bemused. "I can't wait to see how we get along."

Other challenges were more significant. The staff, in particular, faced difficulties with office space in flux. Soon after the church lost its property, it took the opportunity of the change to assess how the staff was doing. The wardens and a team of management analysts interviewed 40 people on the staff. They talked to each person at least an hour. They asked them, "On a scale of 1 to 10, how is your morale?"

Averages are a blunt tool, but the resulting number was blunter still: 4.

The personnel committee needed to take action. Mike Brunner—the husband of Elizabeth Brunner, who had led the pastoral team for years—helped develop a strategy to improve the situation. One clergyman, much beloved in the church, was let go as part of the transition. A church member provided a connection to better office space in a nice modern building. Other staff functions were streamlined. Morale began to improve.

Yates's temporary office was a corner space in the office complex, with windows looking out on trees. The view, at least, was an improvement. Yet something about the situation did not fit. Perhaps corner offices in modern office towers do not usually host such wisdom—and certainly not as much prayer.

A Pruning Season

The church gained from these difficulties. In particular, as the church began considering other properties and opportunities for a new church home, the congregation's vision about its priorities shifted.

On August 26, 2013, over a year after the church had left its old space, Yates reported on a church poll about its future. "I have hundreds and hundreds of wise observations from you, so I can only just summarize some of what you told me." Yates explained that, overall, the church had "a positive assurance that we are in God's hands and being guided." The congregation supported evangelism, the healing ministry, growing maturity, a focus on the next generation, and, as for the priority of finding a new church home, "openness to different sorts of facilities."

The new home needed to meet basic needs and "feel like a church," but the congregation generally seemed "open to something less traditional—the extended Falls Church region is the regional center of our population, but many are willing to be farther out or closer in." Finally, Yates wrote, as the petition to the U.S. Supreme Court was still pending at the time and held out a very slim chance of regaining the historic property, "no one expressed to me a desire to go back to our old facilities but some did suggest that if we ever receive the historic property, we could plant a daughter church there!"

Yates summarized another collective thought of the church, which came in various forms:

We have cut loose from a dependence on our old buildings and this has brought us to a new place as a congregation. You are much less focused on the past and more concerned about living into what God has for us in the future. Somehow our future decisions about a 'home' for us will force us to continue to think in fresh and unorthodox ways about 'church,' and we may need to be willing to take some faith steps that make us uncomfortable or insecure in order to learn the rest that God has to teach us—as some said, we really have to shed worldly thinking and be willing to do 'crazy' things. Not sure what that means but it could be quite true!

This message about property reflected something deeper. People were changing simply by committing to the church throughout the tabernacle season. It started with the vote in 2006, which "made people be real about what they believed," Molly Shafferman said.

In spring 2014, the church hired a new Timothy Fellow, Dan Marotta. When Dan told his friends and colleagues about this, they had different reactions. Some knew about the church and said, *hey, that's great.* Others were not so sure. One said, "that's interesting, you know, that church has been through the ringer. They don't have a building. You sure that's where you want to go?" Another: "the church's heyday is in the past. It's old news."

None of that deterred Dan. He thought, *would I rather go to an old, safe church, or to a church that's putting it on the line for the gospel?* "I don't know of any other church in our country that has lost as much for the gospel," Dan said. "They've been through the fire. The chaff has burned away. That's the body of people I want to learn from. That's where I want to be."

When the church was at the old property, things had seemed buttoned up. Even the newer sanctuary was colonial brick. The aura of prestige drifted through it. On the right Sunday morning, a newcomer might look around and see a bunch of perfect-looking rich people.

Something about a clear and direct loss hits that image hard. The congregation can't be full of perfect winners if they just lost. Losing makes people reflect. It makes them look inside and notice the broken pieces.

"I think it has something to do with pride," Martha Cole said. "The old property was not quite big enough for us, but we loved it. We loved the history and the sense of importance of the place. We never looked at the negatives. We wouldn't have left if God hadn't led us out."

But God did lead the church out, and He used that to make the church a new people. "It released us," Sam Thomsen said. "That property was constraining us."

So now the church had room to grow. The key question was *how* and *where* it would grow.

Yates spoke to this in the spring of 2015:

> I have come to see our great losses of a few years ago as, truthfully, great gains because in the pruning away of so much that was precious to us we have the opportunity to be more fruitful now than we were. Property, programs, plans, people— they all can be like branches that are actually requiring so much attention or needing so much care and feeding that they are reducing the overall fruitfulness of Christ's body. Our father has pruned us of our attitudes and assumptions and obligations and necessities as well as property and programs.
>
> *Yates identified the challenge ahead of not only establishing a new church home, but* "to resist the mindset that might prevent us from bearing fruit. Surely a major question that we must be asking God repeatedly and in connection with so many future decisions is, "Father, will this result in our being more fruitful? Will this lead to the multiplication of true disciples and to the qualities of love, joy, peace, patience, kindness, goodness, gentleness, faithfulness, self-control, and the truth of Christ among us?"

A testament to this fruit was that, during the tabernacle season, the church sent off new daughter churches, and hundreds of members with them. Despite these departures, church attendance dipped only slightly and financial giving increased greatly. That meant new people were coming. And they were people who wanted to join in this journey, difficult as it was.

18

God's Plan Forward

And let them make me a sanctuary, that I may dwell in their midst.
Exactly as I show you concerning the pattern of the tabernacle,
and of all its furniture, so you shall make it.
Exodus 25:8-9

What should a church's focus be when it is preparing to build a new building? Should it be the right architecture to glorify God and make beautiful worship? Or maybe great meeting spaces to conduct the church's affairs? The long journey of The Falls Church Anglican—including its losses—had shifted its focus to transcend these things.

The Forward Campaign

In 2014, the vestry and real estate committee of The Falls Church Anglican, which had been working hard behind the scenes, announced a promising new property. It was not what the congregation might have expected. There was no church building. There were no trees or grassy expanses. There was only a parking lot, a parking garage, and an office building—all situated alongside a major, traffic-congested road.

The church had lost its manicured grounds with tall oaks and peaceful pathways. It had lost its brick, Georgian-style church that George Washington's vestry had commissioned. It had lost the main sanctuary, with its immense organ and hosting capacity, which these people had paid millions for.

Really, someone might think, *we've lost all that, and now all we get is a parking lot, a parking garage, and an office building?*

Yes, exactly. John Yates had previewed this. The church was open to something new. They were open to serving God wherever He called them.

One church member, Suzanne Martinez, made the case for how this secular office building could in fact be in God's plans for the church. "As strange as it may seem to some, purchasing commercial properties to house growing church populations has been a proven ministry model for innovative churches around the country for over three decades."

"Innovative" is not a word used often for Anglican churches. They are known for steadfast loyalty to the 17th-century Book of Common Prayer and its ancient liturgy. And indeed, the churches Suzanne described as examples were not Anglican. They were large evangelical churches in Texas and other places.

These churches, she explained, "have purchased and leased commercial properties such as office buildings, old warehouses, and movie theaters to house their mushrooming church populations." She pointed to the ministry of churches using unusual properties, "not least the drawing into the church of non-believers and allowing creative means of introducing people to Jesus. Often these possibilities include a broader external focus, including extensive community service." These services—from educational programs to medical clinics—enabled many people to connect with the church "long before they attend on a Sunday morning."

Suzanne encouraged the church to heed God's words about what, exactly, the church was supposed to be. The congregation knew now, without a doubt, that "church" was not the colonial building that Washington had once attended. But what was it? Suzanne suggested an answer: "Psalm 24:1 tells us, 'The earth is the Lord's, and everything in it, the world, and all who live in it.' Based on that truth, believers need not draw such a distinction between the sacred and the secular. God's church is His body—us, His people—not a building, be it a traditional church building, secular storefront, office space, or theater. As Moses and the Israelites learned from their 40-year wilderness wandering, we, too, have learned from our recent tabernacle adventure that we can worship and serve Jesus anywhere."

The church agreed to move forward with considering this unusual property. But the proof would come only when wallets had to open. The church gave its members a guide for forty days of prayerful discernment. Members prayed over this property and God's plan.

Then, on November 16, 2014, the church convened a special meeting to vote on whether to buy a new property. The outcome, like the outcome eight years before to leave The Episcopal Church, was crystal clear: 95% voted to move forward.

In the following months, the church members pledged over $24 million to buy the property, and the church proceeded to do so. Plans began to build a new sanctuary, and maybe to create a health and healing center in the office building—reflecting the lessons that the church had learned through both its years of growth and its losses.[70]

It would not be the same as those days in Washington's building. It would never the same. But that's not what Jesus promised. He promised that *He* would stay the same, not that circumstances would. He promised trials and tribulations. And He promised a hope that overcomes, and life everlasting.

Moving Forward in Love

The Falls Church Anglican has found a path leading forward, with its focus on love and the source of love, Jesus Christ.

"We're big," Bill Haley said one Sunday in 2015, "but we're too small." He spoke to the important opportunities of the church's move to a new place. "We need to invite more people into our family."

On a regular Sunday morning in April 2015, the church met at its usual worship spot, Bishop O'Connell High School. Except this time, instead of the plush chairs of the auditorium, the church met in the gymnasium.

It was a gym like any you could find in an American high school. The basketball goals were down. The sun poured in through the bright, sterile space. The church helpers had brought a stage to mid-court. One side of the bleachers was pulled out, and folding chairs filled the space between. It was the perfect setting for a large PTA meeting. But this was a church. This was worship.

At the church's earlier Sunday service, the liturgy and music are more formal. So are the people. More of the church's older members tend to come then. They are wearing suits and have coiffed gray hair.

The misfit is apparent this Sunday morning. These people belong in an established brick colonial church—ideally something Episcopal, with a rich history and a distinguished air. And yet, these people do fit here. They would fit anywhere as long as they are together, worshiping the Lord. When you consider where many of them were thirty years before—young adults fired up for Christ with John Yates in the pulpit—it makes sense. This is a changed people.

As soon as worship starts, this becomes clear. The sound of a cathedral's organ fills the gym. Voices lift together in song. As the music rises, a few old hands lift in praise. Amidst them are younger hands, too. The Millennial generation worshiping beside them, soaking in the same spirit—the Holy Spirit that binds them.

Another remarkable thing about this service is that John Yates is nowhere to be seen. He's still the church's leader. The rector's note on the cover of the bulletin is by him. But it's two Timothy Fellows leading the service.

Sam Ferguson is preaching. Halfway through the service, he rises for the sermon. "If any of you are tempted to shoot hoops, and I can see why it's tempting with these goals behind me, please refrain." The congregation laughs. "It's a blessing to be in the gym," Sam continues, "rather than the auditorium, because I can see all of you."

Sam teaches a lesson on the uniqueness of Christian love. "We love like the incarnation, because of the incarnation." He focuses on 1 John 3, and he explains that God has called us into his family. "See what kind of love the Father has given to us, that we should be called children of God; and so we are." But this isn't a sermon about the *feeling* of love. It's not like the "sea of sentimentality" that our modern culture adores. As always, the word from the pulpit has a counter-cultural grain.

"In the years ahead," Sam says, "we're going to have difficulty." The church will face many choices, and will have plenty of opportunities for strife. "This is the soil where Christian love is shown. It is like a rose growing from those difficulties."

Sam offers a practical point. "Carry a cross, literally. Keep it in your pocket, and ideally a crucifix. When you see someone in the church who is hard to love, rub your fingers over that cross and remember God's love." Sam reads 1 John 3:16: "By this we know love, that he laid down his life for us, and we ought to lay down our lives for the brothers."

Sam looks up. He can see all the faces—these people sitting in a high school gym—and they can see his earnest stare. "Have you seen a crucifix?" he asks. "That's what love looks like."

The Fruits of God's Love

On a winter Sunday in early 2016, the church gathers for another worship service in a high school auditorium. An image of stained glass projects behind the stage in the cavernous and windowless room. Halfway through the service, the time comes for a baptism.

A middle-aged man takes the stage beside John Yates and Robert Watkin. Other church members stand behind him. His name is Ehsan.

Robert Watkin begins to tell Ehsan's story. The man is from Iran, and like many there, from an Islamic faith. Ehsan has long looked for answers to life's deepest questions. He has looked in the Quran, but in it he found a frightening image of God, life, and death. In college he began to read the Bible. He found a different image of God—of unconditional love, even for prostitutes and tax collectors. Ehsan had hated such people. Something within him began to change. Something drew him to Jesus.

But Ehsan was afraid. What would his family think? How would society respond? He grew depressed and confused. He drank and he smoked. Then one day, instead of going to work, he stayed home and slit both wrists with a razor. A close friend sensed something was wrong. He came to Ehsan's home and saved him that day. Ehsan had another chance.

Life moved on. Ehsan married and had a child. He continued to beg God for answers. In September of the year before, Ehsan's doctor suggested a trip to get away for rest and a fresh perspective. That's how Ehsan came to visit Washington, DC. When he arrived, he met an old family friend who happened to be a member of The Falls Church Anglican. The friend invited Ehsan to come with him one Sunday morning.

Standing on stage, Robert Watkin asks Ehsan, "What were your impressions when you first visited?"

Ehsan explains how beautiful it was to see families together. "In Islam, men and women go to the mosque separately and children can't play there. Worship of God is not joyful." But on that visit to The Falls Church Anglican, Ehsan saw joy, including in the music and the prayers. He remembers how Robert prayed for Iran, Sudan, and Saudi Arabia. "In my country, people say, 'Down with the USA!' But here Robert was praying for Iran. I thought, *what did he say?* It showed me what 'love your enemies' means. It affected me deeply."

Ehsan also began taking an ESOL ("English for Speakers of Other Languages") course through the church. The course offered high quality instruction at a low cost. The teacher gave Ehsan and the rest of the class his card. The teacher said, "Here's my number. Call me any time you need anything. If your car breaks down, if you get taken to jail." Ehsan wondered at this generosity. He asked God, *Why are these people so different?*

After Ehsan's first month in Washington ended, he had an

opportunity to stay. One of the leader's of the church's ESOL program welcomed him into their home. "They told me I'm part of the family."

This family's example moved Ehsan deeply. "I saw how kindly they treat their kids. How they respect each other at home. How lovingly they work for Jesus by inviting different people from China, Saudi Arabia, Yemen, Indonesia, and Iran—and introduce them to Jesus. They taught me that love is a decision, not a feeling, so I started texting my wife, 'I love you' and I saw her change."

At another service that Ehsan attended, John Yates taught that Jesus had been a refugee, and he encouraged the church to open its homes to Syrian refugees. Again Ehsan turned to God: *Many Islamic countries don't accept their own brothers and sisters. How could it be possible for people in a church to show love to Muslim refugees?*

On this day of his baptism, speaking before the congregation, Ehsan says: "I found Jesus by you, my brothers and sisters in Christ! I saw a lot of fruit in your lives. I had read the Bible before but I didn't see the words come alive. You showed me they are alive."

Robert has one last question for Ehsan. It's the question that the church would want every person to hear, and an answer it would love for every person to give. Robert asks, "How has your life changed since becoming a Christian?"

Ehsan answered with these words:

Now I feel a sort of light around me. I can see hatred and anger leaving me.

When I trusted Jesus as my Lord I figured out I'm in a business with God. I confess my sin and give him my darkness … and instead he gives me light and peace.

Trusting in Jesus is the best choice I have ever made and now I have figured out the answers to my questions: We come to this world to see the beauty, glory, and mercy of God. We find a huge love that God has given us for free and we freely give it to others. And through Jesus we find a bridge to eternal life, where we will go to a party with God as our host.

God has awakened this sleepy, historic church, and He is using it in the broader Anglican movement and in the mission of His Kingdom. This promises more global engagement, more healing, more grace, and more beauty. And in eternity, it offers hope of what Ehsan envisioned: "a party with God."

THE END

NOTES

1. The prologue tells the historic story of George Washington's role in Truro Parish. It is a recorded fact that he attended the vestry meeting described, and that the vestry concluded the church building was "rotten and unfit for repair." *Near the Falls: Two Hundred Years of The Falls Church*, Rev. Joseph Hodge Alves & Harold Spelman (1969). Ron Chernow's *Washington: A Life* explains that Washington served three terms as church warden—the highest position for a non-clergyman—and bought church pews and contributed funds for gold leaf inscriptions on the altar piece. Other references consulted for this chapter include David McCullough's *1776* and the detailed history provided on the Mount Vernon website.

   From at least 1765, George Washington served two other churches, Christ Church in Alexandria and Old Pohick Church closer to Mt. Vernon. "The two churches are twin sisters; of each Washington was elected Vestryman; in each he was a frequent worshipper." Christ Church was a sister of the Falls Church, though the latter had more prestige at the time. "If tradition can be relied on, the Church at the Falls was the Parish Church, and the one [in Alexandria] 'the Chapel of Ease.' The respective dignity of the two churches is indicated by the comparative emoluments of the office of sexton in the same; for, in the year 1766, Gerrard Tramill, sexton at the Falls Church, receives a salary of five hundred and sixty pounds of tobacco, while John Rhodes, sexton at Alexandria, receives only five hundred pounds of the same article!" *Washington's Church An Historical Sketch of Old Christ Church, Alexandria, Virginia* (1886), at 8. This little book, somewhat like the present one, was published and sold to benefit the church.

2. After the Revolutionary War, the struggle over church property in Virginia pitted "educated Episcopal clergy and gentry against ...

evangelical challengers," including a Baptist "awakening [that] profoundly influenced the politics of church property." Many churches lost their property. As the young nation would learn, no law separating church and state could completely disentangle religion and politics. Thomas E. Buckley, *Evangelicals Triumphant: The Baptists' Assault on the Virginia Glebes, 1786-1801*, The William and Mary Quarterly 45 (1988).

3. Charles A. Stewart, *The Falls Church* (1936), as quoted in *Near the Falls: Two Hundred Years of The Falls Church*, Rev. Joseph Hodge Alves & Harold Spelman (1969), at 35.

4. *Near the Falls: Two Hundred Years of The Falls Church*, Rev. Joseph Hodge Alves & Harold Spelman (1969), at 92. This book's history of the church finishes in 1969.

5. Bob Slosser, *Miracle in Darien* (1979).

6. The story of the families of Jonathan Edwards and his contemporary originated with an 1874 study by sociologist Richard Dugdale. Recent studies have attempted to discredit the facts about the contemporary's family as an exaggeration, particularly because the story has been used negatively by eugenicists. But the numbers offered here are not meant to prove the truth or to say anything about a family's genes. The numbers simply show that a legacy of virtuous living (or the opposite) can be passed down through the generations.

7. John Yates, *The Fruit of the Spirit Is...*, June 29, 1980. When I started this book, I planned to scour through a huge stack of sermons to find the perfect fits for several points. I eventually did read through the sermons, but I was wrong about one thing. I didn't need to read them all to get the key points. In fact, I found perfect excerpts in the very first old sermons I read, and in every single one after that. These sermons are an immense resource. They can be found at www.tfcanglican.org.

8. John Yates, *Just One Thing*, July 20, 1980.

9. John Yates, *The Unchanging Christ*, November 9, 1980.

10. A church welcome pamphlet from the 1980s began with a note from John Yates: "This old building has been loved and used by all sorts and conditions of men, women and children as a place of worship, learning, fellowship and prayer for over two hundred years. . . . It stands today, looking just as it has always looked, as a reminder that the eternal truth of Jesus Christ is unchanged and as powerful and effective today as it has ever been before. Persons convinced of that truth have gone forth from this building into every imaginable sector of society, from the time when the wilderness lay at our doorstep until now when we find ourselves in the midst of a great metropolitan area. At The Falls Church we are seeking to be committed to Jesus Christ, to his Body throughout the world, and to his work in the world. We have found him to be all sufficient to speak to our needs and are convinced that his mission today is crucial to the well being of all people. We welcome you today and invite you to join us in our worship, fellowship and in his mission in the 1980s."

11. John Yates, *Work That Lasts*, August 31, 1980.

12. John Yates, *Caring Enough to Discipline*, August 17, 1980.

13. This section is not a how-to guide on church growth. It simply recounts the experience at The Falls Church. For deeper studies of how Biblical churches grow and bear fruit, three good resources are *Center Church* by Tim Keller, *Nine Marks of a Healthy Church* by Mark Dever, and *The Living Church* by John Stott.

14. John Yates, *A Christian's Influence*, February 8, 1981.

15. John Yates, *In the Deep Water*, February 6, 1983.

16. *Spiritual Renewal Brings Booming Growth To Three Episcopal Churches In Northern Virginia*, Christianity Today, January 13, 1984 (emphasis added).

17. John Yates, *The Second Commandment - Our Own Idols*, September 26, 1982.

18. John Yates, *Three Marriages and a Funeral*, September 7, 2003.

19. John Yates, *Coathangers, Cockroaches, and George*, September 18, 1983.

20. John Yates, *His Mission Before Us*, July 26, 1981.

21. John Yates, *Making Christ King in the Lives of Others*, November 20, 1983.

22. Learn more about the national Fellows Initiative at www.thefellowsinitiative.org.

23. *In Re: Multi-Circuit Episcopal Church Property Litigation* (CL 2007-0248724), Letter Opinion on the Applicability of Va. Code § 57-9(A), at 4 (April 3, 2008) (quoting Deposition of Bishop-Elect David Anderson).

24. 36 U.S.C. § 119.

25. *A New Christianity For a New World*, available at http://johnshelbyspong.com/.

26. Thaddeus Barnum, *Never Silent*, 103-104 (2008).

27. Barnum, *Never Silent* at 132 (quoting the Rev. Dr. John Rodgers, former dean of Trinity School for Ministry).

28. *See, e.g.*, Genesis 2:23-25; Leviticus 18:22; Romans 1:24-27; 1 Corinthians 6:9-1 & 10:13. For a response to arguments that the Bible supports same-sex relationships, see Tim Keller's article at http://redeemer.com/redeemer-report/article/the_bible_and_same_sex_relationships_a_review_article.

29. John Yates, *The Lord's Last Words*, June 14, 1981.

30. John Yates, *Is Jesus Really Coming Again?*, November 15, 1981.

31. Obituary of Bishop Walter Righter, Pittsburgh Post-Gazette, September 13, 2011.

32. John Yates, *Discipleship, Sexual Purity and the Church Today*, July 14, 1996.

33. Barnum, *Never Silent*, at 106.

34. Barnum, *Never Silent* at 106 (quoting the Philadelphia Enquirer Magazine).

35. This statement appeared on the website of the American Anglican Council. *See* Gary Warth, *Left behind: Episcopalians carry on after church, priest change affiliation*, San Diego Union-Tribune, August 25, 2006.

36. Andrew Carey, *Church of England Newspaper*, July 10, 1998.

37. Resolution 2000-D039, *Acknowledge Relationships Other Than Marriage and Existence of Disagreement on the Church's Teaching*, General Convention, *Journal of the General Convention of The Episcopal Church*, Denver, 2000 (New York: General Convention, 2001), p. 287f.

38. Barnum, *Never Silent*, at 193-194.

39. *Still Fighting over Nicea*, Christianity Today, February 18, 2005.

40. Rowan Williams, *Our Differences Need Not Destroy Us*, April 8, 2000.

41. John Yates, *The Book of Acts: When Good People Disagree*, February 18, 1996.

42. *Heresy Better Than Schism?*, Washington Times, January 31, 2004.

43. As John Yates told a reporter at the New York Times, "The Episcopalian ship is in trouble. So we're climbing over the rails down to various little lifeboats. There's a lifeboat from Bolivia, one from Rwanda, another from Nigeria. Their desire is to help us build a new ship in North America, and design it and get it sailing." *Episcopalians Are Reaching Point of Revolt*, New York Times, December 17, 2006.

44. John Yates, *Can We Trust the Scripture?*, October 19, 2003.

45. Michael Gerson, *Missionaries in Northern Virginia*, Washington Post, May 16, 2007.

46. Martyn Minns, *The Church is Flat: A New Anglicanism*, May 30, 2007.

47. A complete copy of the report by the Reconciliation Commission is available at http://www.standfirminfaith.com/media/diova_reconciliation_commission_report.pdf.

48. *In Re: Multi-Circuit Episcopal Church Property Litigation* (CL 2007-0248724), Letter Opinion on the Applicability of Va. Code § 57-9(A), at 12-13 (April 3, 2008).

49. Barnum, *Never Silent* at 251.

50. Barnum, *Never Silent* at 161.

51. The local press reported this letter, as well as a letter from John Yates to the church recognizing that "there is always risk in

contested lawsuits." *Voting Begins Sunday on Pulling Out Of Denomination at F.C. Episcopal*, Falls Church News-Press (Dec. 6, 2006).

52. *F.C. Episcopal Church Faces Fight to Keep Property After Voting to Exit Denomination*, Falls Church News-Press (Nov. 21, 2006).

53. John Yates, *On Being People of Truth and Grace*, December 17, 2006.

54. Laurie Goodstein, *Episcopalians Are Reaching Point of Revolt*, New York Times, December 17, 2006.

55. Michelle Boorstein, *Moderate Bishop Takes Unexpected Turn*, Washington Post, February 16, 2007.

56. *Editorial: Descent Into The Abyss*, Falls Church News-Press, December 13, 2006.

57. Jeff Chu, *10 Questions for Katharine Jefferts Schori*, Time Magazine, July 10, 2006.

58. Robin Young, *Interview with Katharine Jefferts Schori*, National Public Radio, November 1, 2006.

59. Deborah Solomon, *Questions for Katharine Jefferts Schori, State of the Church*, New York Times, November 19, 2006.

60. Mollie Hemingway, *Twenty-First Century Excommunication*, Wall Street Journal, Oct. 7, 2011.

61. Mollie Hemingway, *Twenty-First Century Excommunication*, Wall Street Journal, Oct. 7, 2011 (emphasis added).

62. Jamie Dean, *Tidings of Discomfort and Joy*, World Magazine, December 13, 2013.

63. *Protestant Episcopal Church v. Truro Church*, July 10, 2010, http://www.courts.state.va.us/opinions/opnscvwp/1090682.pdf. The decision recognized that there had been a division between the Episcopal Church and the departing churches within the Diocese of Virginia, but found that the departing churches were not a "branch" of either the Episcopal Church or the Diocese such that the statute would apply. *Id.* at 29.

64. *The Falls Church v. The Protestant Episcopal Church*, at 24, April 18, 2013.

65. *Editorial: Big Victory for Civil Rights*, Falls Church News-Press, January 12, 2012. Two years later, the same local writer would described "the Yates faction" as "governed by a self-serving, bullying arrogance and chauvinism that ranged from indifference to hate toward all who did not share its views." *Church Defectors Acted Immorally, Part 4*, Falls Church News-Press, April 2, 2014. Such characterizations do not require response, but can simply be compared to the words of John Yates and others throughout this book. The discrepancy becomes apparent.

66. *A Thousand Amens*, available at www.tfcmusic.org.

67. Emily Belz, *A Great Divorce*, World Magazine, June 16, 2012.

68. Emily Belz, *A Great Divorce*, World Magazine, June 16, 2012.

69. *Editorial: The Real Falls Church*, Falls Church News-Press, January 31, 2007.

70. At the time of this writing, the church has completed tentative conceptual designs for the new sanctuary. If the building proceeds with God's blessing, it will announce His presence on a busy corridor into the nation's capital, which previously has had no other church presence. A conceptual design image for the new sanctuary appears on the following page.

THE FALLS CHURCH ANGLICAN

*Conceptual design for new sanctuary of The Falls Church Anglican,
to be built on a busy corridor leading into Washington, D.C.*

OTHER WORKS BY J.B. SIMMONS

Light in the Gloaming
Breaking the Gloaming

Unbound
Clothed with the Sun
Great White Throne

Readers praise *Unbound* as a thrilling page-turner—"the Da Vinci Code meets Hunger Games meets Left Behind."

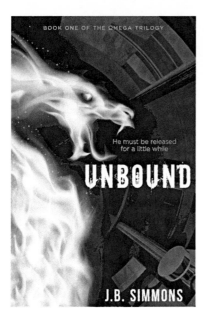

He must be released for a little while.
But the one who sees doesn't believe.

Elijah Goldsmith has nightmares he needs to ignore. Why would a rich kid from Manhattan dream three straight nights about a dragon and the destruction of St. Peter's Basilica? He's never even been to Rome.

This is 2066, the year the world ends.

To get a free copy of *Unbound* and to learn more about other works by J.B. Simmons, visit www.jbsimmons.com.

CPSIA information can be obtained
at www.ICGtesting.com
Printed in the USA
LVOW07*2305200817
545749LV00001B/9/P